An Introduction to Ukrainian Dialectology

WIENER SLAWISTISCHER ALMANACH
LINGUISTISCHE REIHE

Herausgegeben von
Tilmann Reuther

SONDERBAND 94

PETER LANG

Salvatore Del Gaudio

An Introduction
to Ukrainian Dialectology

PETER LANG

Bibliografische Information der Deutschen Nationalbibliothek
Die Deutsche Nationalbibliothek verzeichnet diese Publikation
in der Deutschen Nationalbibliografie; detaillierte bibliografische
Daten sind im Internet über http://dnb.d-nb.de abrufbar.

Umschlagkarte:
https://upload.wikimedia.org/wikipe-
dia/commons/f/f8/Map_of_Ukrainian_dialects_en.png
© Gesellschaft zur Förderung Slawistischer Studien
Alle Rechte vorbehalten

ISSN 0256-5234
ISBN 978-3-631-73812-2 (Print)
E-ISBN 978-3-631-73813-9 (E-Book)
E-ISBN 978-3-631-73814-6 (EPUB)
E-ISBN 978-3-631-73815-3 (MOBI)
DOI 10.3726/b12421

© Peter Lang GmbH
Internationaler Verlag der Wissenschaften
Frankfurt am Main 2017

Diese Publikation wurde begutachtet.
www.peterlang.com

CONTENTS

CHAPTER 3

Preface

The idea of writing an introduction to Ukrainian dialectology in a widely understood European language originated in 2006 when I first began to conduct field work in Ukraine. Although at the time I was not directly working with dialects but on the related social phenomenon of Ukrainian-Russian mixed speech ("suržyk"), I realized that most reference manuals on dialectology were quite obsolete, although still informative.

Secondly, without a sound knowledge of Ukrainian, it was difficult to read existing manuals and to become familiar with Ukrainian dialectal concepts and terminology.

For several years, various reasons forced me to postpone my original plan to supply the students of Ukrainian with the first basic English account on Ukrainian dialectology. In the meantime, a series of new introductions to Ukrainian dialectology have finally been published in Ukraine. Nonetheless I hope that my introduction will still be a useful aid to foreign Ukrainianists.

I wish to thank Dawn Marley (University of Surrey, England) for having patiently proof-read my text, Rudolf Muhr (University of Graz, Austria) who was the very first person who read the manuscript, Andriy Danylenko (Pace University, New York) for the precious advice on some specific content issues, Natalija Verbyč (Institute of Ukrainian Language, Department of dialectology, Ukrainian Academy of Sciences) for having checked the dialectal facts. A final word of appreciation goes to Tilmann Reuther (University of Klagenfurt, Austria) for having always supported my publications.

Kyiv, December 2016

Introductory remarks

The reasons which led me to write an introduction to Ukrainian dialectology are multifold. The main motivation was to render available to a wide range of students of Slavic languages, and particularly of Ukrainian, an outline of Ukrainian dialectology and its dialects. The lack of introductory accounts of Ukrainian dialects in more accessible western European languages represents a great limit to all those students of Slavic languages who wish to approach the fascinating world of geographical variation of contemporary Ukrainian. All manuals on Ukrainian dialects in fact, with the exception of a limited number of short American and German contributions, are written in Ukrainian. This represents an obvious hindrance to students of Ukrainian, whose initial level does not always allow a deep understanding of the contents of these books. A basic knowledge of Ukrainian dialects is important to complete the theoretical and practical background of a Slavist, especially if studying the Eastern group of Slavic languages (Russian, Belarusian, Ukrainian).

A knowledge of territorial variation is a valuable aid to a better understanding of diachronic (historical variation and its reflection in documents of various geographic provenance) and synchronic language processes. Additionally it helps to better assess some contemporary sociolinguistic issues and various forms of language/dialectal mixture such as, for example, the Ukrainian-Russian mixed speech "suržyk".

With the purpose of filling this theoretical and practical gap, this guidebook aims to elaborate on the existing dialectological data with some recent studies on the topic. In

7

the main, though, the illustrative material relies on traditional Ukrainian works and on a small number of English and German sources.

This introduction is similarly meant to facilitate the task of those scholars working in related fields who are looking for some basic facts about Ukrainian dialects. It can also be of interest to the layman who simply wishes to gain an insight into Ukrainian dialectology.

At the same time, the book could be used as a support to a reader in Slavic languages approaching this complex research field for the first time. However, this introduction is not addressed to those professional Ukrainianists who have already acquired a solid background in Ukrainian dialectology and in Ukrainian Studies.

The manual is organized into three parts. The first one, after an outline of the Ukrainian language for non-specialists, will introduce the main issues of Ukrainian dialectology.

The second part will exemplify the Ukrainian dialectal territory and the most typical features of the main dialectal areas.

The final part will introduce and briefly discuss some contemporary issues such as the relation between dialects and forms of language mix; the relation between dialectology and sociolinguistics in the Ukrainian linguistic tradition, and the question of the 'Rusyn' language.

A glossary of the most frequent Ukrainian dialectal terms with their English equivalents concludes the book. Illustrative materials are provided contextually. Reference works on dialectology can be found in the final bibliography. The Cyrillic titles of reference books have not been transliterated into Latin characters to enable their rapid indentification.

For the sake of clarity, we have mainly avoided the use of abbreviations as is often customary in linguistic publications. The only abbreviations concern the verbal aspect -

imperf. stands for 'imperfective' and perf. for 'perfective';
prep. means preposition; the cases: nom., gen., dat., acc.,
instr., loc., voc. respectively stand for nominative, genitive,
dative, accusative, instrumental, locative, vocative.
Ukrainian geographical names (toponyms) have been rendered according to the scientific transliteration system, for
example, the place name Kyiv (official variant)[1] has been
transliterated as Kyjiv.
Some ancient ethnonyms which refer to east Slavic tribes
have been anglicized, e.g. *Polians* instead of *Poljane* as
used in Shevelov (1979). The classification of dialects partially relies on the traditional English spelling established
by Shevelov (ibid.); in the case of those dialects spoken in
the area of the river Dnipro however, the denomination
Dnipro dialects has been preferred to the more traditional
Dnieper dialects.
The description of dialectal facts is limited to the essential
features of each macro-dialectal area. This is particularly
true for south-western dialects which show a higher degree
of local variation. This choice is easily explained if one considers the introductory character of the present work.
It is known that dialects undergo visible changes within a
few decades, especially as a consequence of standardization
processes. They may be either affected by standard Ukrainian or, in specific geographical areas, by Russian or other
languages (e.g. Polish, Hungarian, Belarusian etc.). For this
reason, the correctness and topicality of certain dialectal
data need to be proved regularly.

---

[1] Kiev is the form based on Russian but it is still widely used.

NOTES

0. The Ukrainian language[2]

Standard Ukrainian[3], according to the traditional subdivision of the Slavic languages, belongs to the East Slavic language group along with Russian and Belarusian. The historical criteria for a classification of East Slavic languages essentially rely on common phonetic-phonological outcomes and, to a lesser extent, on morphological ones. Modern Ukrainian and Russian languages present substantial differences in phonetics, syntax and lexis. Belarusian is

---

[2] This outline, as mentioned in the introductory lines, is meant for non-specialist readers. The most essential facts about the Ukrainian language are reported. It may appear obvious to an advanced student of Slavic languages but it is not always so evident for the majority of readers or even linguists.

[3] Besides the term "Ukrainian" (cf. "ukrajins'ka literaturna mova") which has established itself as the main ethnonym in the last two centuries, there are a series of historical denominations based on the root RUS', for example: *rus'kyj jazyk* or *rus'ka mova* etc. The adjective *rus'kij*, (cf. Rusian), designated for many centuries (X-XVII) the historical regions of contemporary Ukraine, whereas the language spoken by those East Slavs now living on the territory of present day Russia were often referred to as Muscovian. The term "Russian" to mean the language spoken by the inhabitants of Russia became prevalent only starting with the epoch of Peter I in the 18th century. In the 19th century, for a number of socio-political and historical reasons, which will not discussed here, the term "Little Russians" which had been used to designate Ukrainians since earlier epochs, began to take on a specific connotation. In that period the Russians were called "Great Russians" and the Belarusians – "White Russians". In the 19th century dialectal tradition, Russian was used as a hyperonym to mean all East Slavic vernaculars. Cfr. Pivtorak (2004: 69-83). http://litopys.org.ua/rizne/ukrtable.htm (07.02.2015).

11

historically and typologically closer to Ukrainian. To this classification, some scholars add Rusyn, which for others is just a western Ukrainian dialectal variety claiming the status of a language.[4]

Ukrainian is the only official language of the Ukrainian state which gained independence from the Soviet Union in 1991. The calculation of its native speakers varies according to the census and the criteria used in the sociological and sociolinguistic surveys. The number of Ukrainian native speakers fluctuates between approx. 38 million (about 73%) out of a population of 52 million Ukrainian citizens[5], and 45 million native speakers as reported in the Encyclopedia of the Ukrainian Language (2004: 716). This number undoubtedly increases if one considers the large Ukrainian emigrant communities who live in a large number of countries round the world.

The 2001 census fixed the Ukrainian population at about 48.5 million inhabitants: 67.5 % of the population declared Ukrainian as mother tongue; 29.6 % Russian and 3% other languages.

According to the sociolinguistic parameters used in the survey, Ukrainian can either be classified as the second most widely spoken Slavic language after Russian or as the third most widespread language after Russian and Polish. The estimation of these figures may vary because of the high emigration rate of the last two decades. Nonetheless Ukrainian is among the 30 most spoken languages worldwide.[6] Ukrainian enjoys the status of a regional language in Transnistria, Poland, Romania, Slovakia, Serbia, Croa-

---

4 See: Section 3.2.

5 Cf. Danylenko & Vakulenko (1995: 1); Schweier (1998: 94).

6 http://langs.com.ua/movy/demogr.htm;
   http://www.vistawide.com/languages/top_30_languages.htm;
   http://photius.com/rankings/languages2.html (07.02.2015).

tia, Bosnia. As mentioned, it is largely spoken in many mi-
grant communities around the world, in particular: Canada, USA, Brazil; in Europe: Portugal, Greece, Spain and
Italy.[7]
Standard Ukrainian is regulated by the National Academy
of Sciences of Ukraine, particularly by its Institute of
Ukrainian Language (Instytut ukrajins'koji movy), Ukrainian language-information fund, and the Potebnja Institute
of Linguistics (Instytut Movoznavstva).
Standard Ukrainian retains a varying degree of mutual intelligibility with Belarusian, Russian and other Slavic languages. It is lexically closer to Belarusian with around 84%
of common vocabulary than to Russian with which, according to certain surveys[8], it only shares 62% of common
vocabulary. With Polish standard Ukrainian shares about
70% of common lexemes.
In reality, the percentage of common lexical items Ukrainian shares with either Russian, Polish or Slovak also de-
pends on the dialectal areas. Therefore, the percentage of
vocabulary shared with Russian may be significantly
higher especially in the north-east and south-east of the
country.
Furthermore, the majority of ethnic Ukrainians who de-
clare Ukrainian as their mother tongue, for well-known
historical, socio-political and sociolinguistic reasons, show
a high command of Russian. In certain areas of the country the fluency and knowledge of Russian is comparable to

---

[7] For an overview of the Ukrainian language in Italy, see: Del Gaudio (2012).

[8] Cf. Мови Європи: відстані між мовами за словниковим складом (Languages of Europe: distances according to the vocabulary
composition).
http://journal.mandrivets.com
/images/file/Tyshchenko_2010_3.pdf

that of a native speaker, while in others it is limited to a kind of second language.

The Russian used in Ukraine by the majority of its speakers is characterized by a series of idiosyncrasies which lead contemporary sociolinguists to speak of an emerging 'national' variety of Russian, also known as Ukrainian-Russian.[9]

At the same time a series of minority languages coexist, along with Ukrainian, in some parts of the country, e.g. Rumanian in its Moldavian variety, Hungarian etc.

Finally the existence of a Ukrainian-Russian mixed speech, known as suržyk[10], and the interaction between dialects and different language varieties render the language situation of Ukraine at the same time interesting but confusing to an external observer.

The two maps[11] below will respectively show:
1) the areas where Ukrainian and varieties based on Ukrainian are spoken;

---

[9] Its status is still unclear and is the object of debates. It is however undeniable that the Russian used by the average speaker in Ukraine visibly differs from that of Russia. See: Del Gaudio (2012); Del Gaudio & Ivanova (2015b).

[10] We shall return later to this point. Cf. Section 3.1.

[11] The purpose of Map 1 is to highlight the respective areas regardless of specific etnonyms, cf. https://upload. wikimedia. org/wikipedia/commons/a/aa/Ukrainians_en.svg.
The languages indicated with different colours in Map 2 have a mere indicative function, i.e. the official language is Ukrainian (or was Ukrainian before the recent events of 2014-2015) throughout the country. Other "minority" languages coexist along with standard Ukrainian, Ukrainian dialectal varieties and different forms of language mix on the highlighted territories. Forms of language mix are not only the Ukrainian-Russian mixed speech "suržyk" or Russian with Ukrainian admixture but also Ukrainian with admixture of other languages, e.g. Polish, Rumanian etc. cf. http://russia-insider.com/en/politics/you-think-lot-people-ukraine-speak-ukrainian-think-again/ri1007.

14

2)other major languages spoken along with Ukrainian.

Map 1: Ukrainians and Ukrainian based varieties

Map 2: Languages spoken in Ukraine

NOTES

CHAPTER 1

1. Dialectology: basic concepts

In a generalized way one can define dialectology (from Greek διάλεκτος, *dialektos*, "talk, dialect"; the particle διά implies separation, diversification, variation and -λογία, - *logia* "word, study") as the discipline which studies the dialects of a specific language. The term dialect was first coined in 1577 on the basis of a Graeco-Latin term *dialectus* (διάλεκτος), i.e. *way of speaking of specific people*. Dialectal variation is present in most language areas and often has important social implications. The study of dialects deals with the variant features within a language, their history, differences of form and meaning, distribution, and, more generally, the spoken as distinct from their literary forms. The discipline recognizes all variations within the boundaries of any given language; it classifies and interprets them according to historical origins, principles of development, characteristic features, areal distribution, and social correlates.[12]

The Encyclopedia of Ukrainian defines dialectology as the branch of linguistics which studies:

a) the dialectal language;
b) its spatial (diatopic) variation and territorial differentiation;
c) the history of language-territorial formation and specific language phenomena;

---

[12] http://www.encyclopedia.com/doc/1O29-DIALECTOLOGY.html

d) the relation and interaction between other forms of existence of the language of the ethnic group, for example: literary language, *prostoriččja* and social dialects".[13]

The spoken language, particularly in its territorial and rural dimension, not only preserves the current state of the language but also those language elements which are no longer in use or are dying out (archaic features or language relics); it may sometimes contain innovative features and neologisms. At the same time elements of different dialects or of the standard language may co-exist at dialectal level. Each language/dialectal element has its own territorial diffusion called **area** (Ukr. ареал). A dialect is a territorial-linguistic formation combining areas which include different levels of dialectal elements. A dialect is delimited on a linguistic map by a bunch of isoglosses.

An **isogloss** is a conventional line on a map marking an area having a distinct linguistic feature. Moreover, dialects often share elements common to other languages, particularly if these are cognate.

The definition of "dialect" and the distinction between "dialect and language" are not always as easy as may appear at first sight, or as certain western European dialectal traditions seem to imply.

The Oxford Concise Dictionary of Linguistics (1997: 96-97) defines a dialect as "any distinct variety of a language, especially one spoken in a specific part of a country or other geographical area".

---

[13] For the sake of clearness, we have broken up the definition in points. Here the original citation: "Діалектологія – розділ мовознавства, що вивчає діалектну мову, її просторову варіативність і територіальну диференціацію, історію формування мовно-територіальних утворень і окремих мовних явищ, співвідношення та взаємодію з іншими формами існування мови етносу — літературною, просторіччям, соціальними діалектами" (Hrycenko 2004: 149).

Chapter 1

Crystal speaks of regional or socially distinctive variety of language, blending the geographic dimension with the social one. For the reasons just expressed, dialectology, also 'linguistic geography' or dialect geography, is defined as "the systematic study of all forms of dialect, but especially **regional** dialect", where the regional and geographic components are being emphasized (Cf. Crystal 2008: 142-143). In contrast with the tendency typical of the English speaking countries of fusing the later findings of sociolinguistics (social dialectology) with the geo-linguistic approach of traditional dialectology, in the east Slavic dialectological tradition, the two disciplines are clearly kept separated and the diatopic dimension is still dominant.[14]

Apart from the famous saying that "a dialect is a language without an army and a navy", a few criteria have been suggested to distinguish dialects from languages.

A widely accepted framework adopted in west European (Anglo-American) dialectology relies on three criteria that may, in some instances, contradict one another. These can be summed up in the following points:

1. Mutual intelligibility;
2. Cultural criterion;
3. Political status.

Mutual intelligibility is one of the most accredited criteria, although not the only one and not always appropriate. One assumes that a speaker from one part of a country will be able to understand someone from another geographical area of the same country and within the boundaries of the same national language. Within this perspective, language is seen as a collection of mutually intelligible dialects. The reality is more complex. There are cases of mutual intelligibility, or at least some degree of it, among

---

[14] We shall return to this point in section 3.3.

different official languages, e.g. Scandinavian; some Slavic languages, e.g. Belarusian and Ukrainian) etc.; between some Romance languages, for example Italian and Spanish. On the other hand, there are cases where dialects of a single national language are not mutually intelligible. Italian dialects, for example, may not be mutually intelligible from one end to another of the Italian Peninsula. Furthermore, mutual intelligibility may not be equal in both directions (Chambers & Trudgill 1998: 3-4). This may often depend on the inclination, level of education, linguistic sensibility and language exposure of a speaker of a certain language and/or variety to a similar one.

Another fundamental concept related to the criterion expressed above is that of **dialect continuum**: within a language, speakers of Dialect A can understand and be understood by speakers of Dialect B, and C by B, and so on, but at the extremes of the continuum speakers of A and Z may be mutually unintelligible. The A and Z communities may therefore feel justified in supposing or arguing that A and Z are different languages. If politics intervenes and the speakers of A and Z come to be citizens of different countries, the dialects may well be socially revalued as 'languages' (in due course with their own dialects and standard variety).[15] If language differences cause only minimal problems in communication, there is a tendency to call this discrepancy varieties of a single language: such is the case with British English, Australian English, American English; Russian in the Russian Federation and in some post-Soviet states, e.g. Ukrainian Russian, Belarusian Russian etc. or German in Austria, Switzerland, Germany. The **cultural criterion** takes into account the opinion of speakers and how these consider their language variety in relation to a more standard form of speech. This could also

---

[15] Cf. http://www.encyclopedia.com/topic/dialect.aspx#1-1029: DIALECT-full.

be the already mentioned case of Scandinavian languages
which show a high degree of mutual intelligibility. Nevertheless, a very small number of Danes or Norwegians
would claim, for example, that their language is a substandard dialect of Swedish. Each language – Danish, Nor-
wegian, Swedish, Icelandic – has its own, separate literary
standard, even though the language forms themselves
show a fairly high degree of mutual intelligibility. A similar
situation could be observed for Ukrainian in relation to
Belarusian or to some of the Slavic languages of former
Yugoslavia.

The **political status** attributed to a particular variety is
also a criterion in differentiating language from dialect.
This factor is external to the form of the language and
sometimes even in conflict with the culture of the speakers. There are cases in which languages which are not mutually intelligible, or only partially, may be called dialects
simply because they are spoken within a single political
entity and this leads the rulers of that particular state to
consider them as such. This was, for example, the case
with Ukrainian and Russian in the days of the Russian
Empire, where Ukrainian (known as Little Russian) was
considered a substandard variety of Russian (known as
Great Russian). This could also be said to be the case with
the so-called dialects of Chinese in the People's Republic
of China.[16]

For all these reasons, it is useful, often for practical purposes, to regard certain varieties as **dialects** of a **language**
(Cf. Chambers & Trudgill 1984: 3).

A dialect that it is related and regarded as a subdivision of
a particular language is endowed with its own system and
fulfills the communicative function among the people of

---

[16] Cf. http://pandora.cii.wwu.edu/vajda/ling201/test3materials/
dialectology.htm.

this territory. It has its own 'norm', although the latter is less stable than that of the standard language.

The distinction between a dialect and a language seems to have been of minor concern in Ukrainian, and more widely, East Slavic dialectal literature.[17] In most reference books in fact there is no explicit reference to the criteria which would differentiate a 'dialect' from a 'language'. Notwithstanding this shortcoming, a specific Ukrainian and East Slavic framework seems to rely on two basic criteria:

1) Structural criteria (структурні критерії);
2) Historical-cultural criteria (історико-культурні критерії).

As to the **structural-functional criteria**, one can say that a dialect is the language spoken on a specific territory endowed, just like any language, with structural and systemic features. It fulfils the people's communicative needs and functions on a determinate territory. Dialect has its own micro-norm, which is less stable and subject to change compared with the standard language.[18] The **structural criteria** imply a hierarchy: from the smallest unit (hovir) to a larger dialectal entity.[19] The former is considered to be a less rigid language microsystem which is territorially confined to one, or more rarely, two local settlements.

The **historical-cultural criteria** involve extra-linguistic factors such as the sense of belonging to a particular language and its cultural group (ethnic language consciousness) and the conditions which historically affected a par-

---

[17] Personal consultation with Hrycenko (director of the department of Ukrainian dialectology and the Institute of the Ukrainian Language, Ukrainian Academy of Sciences).

[18] In the East Slavic tradition, the term "literary language" stands for standard.

[19] This point will be discussed in detail in section 1.3.

ticularly territory, its geo-political boundaries and its culture. This point partially overlaps with the "cultural criterion" already discussed in connection with the west European framework.

Besides the two basic criteria mentioned above, a third criterion sometimes suggested in East Slavic dialectology to distinguish a dialect from a language is the **degree of literacy**.[20] According to this criterion, dialects, by definition, are characterized by the absence of an independent written language; a writing system is either non-existent or very limited, and it is often based on the standard language. There is no literary production with the exception of some folk songs, proverbs, sayings and some individual poetic forms. Nevertheless if this criterion can be applied to specific dialect situations and it seems to work for the East Slavic dialects in which a dialect is in essence a territorially limited oral speech variety with a restricted or non-existent literary tradition, the same cannot be said of other language realities.[21]

Accepting the widely acknowledged definition that dialectology is the study of a language in its territorial (vernacular) forms, some dialectological approaches distinguish:

  1) territorial dialects;
  2) social dialects.

Territorial dialects presuppose variation in space (territory), whereas the speech specificity of social and/or professional groups is called a social dialect. However, dialectology, as a descriptive branch of linguistics, traditionally investigates and describes territorial dialects.

---

[20] http://files.school-collection.edu.ru/dlrstore/b73c2872-433e-7854-175c-94b0c9156a9e/1007720A.htm.

[21] In the Romance language areas, especially on the Italian territory, for example, most of the so called "dialects" have their own literary traditions.

Chapter 1

1.1. Dialectology as a discipline

The scientific study of dialects in Europe dates from around the mid-19th century, when philologists using data preserved in texts began to work out the historical or diachronic development of the Indo-European languages. Early dialectologists were particularly interested in lexical variation. Aims and research objects of early dialectology often overlap with the tasks of language history and historic grammar. In the second half of the 19th century, dialectology benefitted from the research methods of linguistic geography and cartography.

It is generally possible to identify at least two bases for dialectology. Dialectology is considered as "a natural outgrowth of the comparative study of language differences and similarities across both time and space" (Francis 1983: 48). Another view is that dialectology begins from dialect geography, a discipline established by scholars such as Georg Wenker (1876) and Jules Gilliéron (1897-1901) in the late 19th century. These early researchers gave the impulse for the development of most of the national dialectal surveys in Italy[22], southern Switzerland, Spain, England and other countries in the following decades. Dialect geography as a discipline experienced rapid success until the mid-20th century.

From the 1960s onwards, the fervent dialectological activity, with some exceptions, began to modify its original research objectives. Dialect research took a new direction,

---

[22] A milestone in Italian dialectology was marked by Bondelli's *Essay on Gallo-Italic Dialects* (original title: *Saggio sui dialetti gallo italici*) written in 1853-1854. The essay is not only important for the further development of the substrate theory but also because it assumes the 'autonomy' of dialects which are considered as separate units, and not subordinate to a particular language. His work also paid attention to social variability and is characterized by the initiative to document dialects with field work surveys (cf. Grassi, Sobrero, Telmon 1997: 37-47).

focusing on urban dialectology rather than rural. This change can be explained by a series of interrelated factors such as criticisms of the way dialectological data were being collected, the development of new technology in recording data (tape-recorder), the rise of sociolinguistics as a strictly related discipline.[23] As to critics, it was argued, firstly, that dialectology should not just be interested in a very small proportion of the population, i.e. old, rural and male, but also include the young, women and those living in towns and cities.

Secondly, critics argued that one-word answers to questionnaires[24] were too distant from everyday language to provide a really accurate account of how people used language. They suggested that dialectology should study continuous and relaxed conversation which not only would provide examples of more everyday language but also highlight variability within the speech of the individual. Moreover, a practical hindrance to the further development of large dialect-geography surveys has to do with the lack of appropriate financing along with the difficulty in finding capable and enthusiastic practitioners (Cf. Chambers and Trudgill 1984: 23-35).

In the part of Ukraine which was subject to the Russian empire, an impulse to the development of dialectology was given by the advance of Russian dialectology in the 19th century. In this period the first fragmented descriptions of dialectal facts began to be published. This was connected with a renewed ethnographic interest in the everyday life of

---

[23] The relation between dialectology and sociolinguistics will not be discussed here since it goes beyond the scope of this introduction.

[24] In most cases long questionnaires were used, with survey workers asking usually non-mobile, old, rural men (NORMs) to respond, usually with one-word answers, to questions such as: 'You sweeten tea with.....?' and 'What do you say to a caller at the door if you want him to enter?' The answers to the questions were then transcribed phonetically by the survey worker.

country people. If the attitude towards dialects had been negative in the first half of the 19ᵗʰ century, by the mid-nineteenth century dialects were nolonger considered a "distortion" of the literary language; on the contrary a sense of respect towards the way of speaking of country people began to prevail. The publication of the *Explanatory Dictionary of the Spoken Great Russian Language* (*Tolkovyj slovar' živogo velikorusskogo jazyka*, 1863-1866) by Dal' undoubtedly played an important role in the evaluation of dialects. This dictionary, which contains about two hundred thousand entries, recorded about eighty thousand dialectal words including Ukrainian and Belarusian.

A further step towards the establishement of dialectology as an independent research branch within the Russian empire was provided by the substantial contributions of Karskij (1860-1931), Šachmatov (1864-1920), and the work of the Moscow Dialectological Commission (MDK).[25] One of the main achivements of this linguistic circle was the drawing of the first "dialectal map of the Russian language" (Ušakov, Durnovo, Sokolov, 1915) which included the Ukrainian and Belarusian dialectal territories.[26]

1.2. Studies on Ukrainian dialects

Ukrainian dialectology is no exception to the general framework presented above. It began to take shape as a discipline around the middle of the 19ᵗʰ century within the framework of the Russian linguistic tradition.[27] There were also attempts at describing specific dialectal characteristics prior to this period; for example Šafons'kyj in the second half of the 18th century (Hrycenko 2004: 150).

---

[25] For more details on this point, see: Jakobson (1971: 530ff.); Kasatkin et al. (2005: 12-13).

[26] At that time the term 'Russian' was often used as a hyperonym to mean East Slavic.

[27] See: previous note.

Early studies of specific dialectal phenomena were not sys-
tematically carried out. One of the main concerns of dialectology was the classification and genetic explanation of
dialectal facts. In the second half of the 19th century,
thanks to the contributions of linguists and dialectologists
such as Potebnja, Mychal'čuk[28] (1877) and others, Ukrainian dialectology gradually acquired the status of an independent discipline.
In the first part of the 20th century a decisive contribution
to the development of Ukrainian dialectology was given by
the works of Vsevolod Hancov (1924; 1925) and Olena
Kurylo (1924; 1925; 1928).[29] The collection of dialectal
data was carried out on the basis of largely discussed
questionnaires elaborated by Kryms'kyj, Tymčenko, Larin.
The methodology of dialectal studies changed substantially during the last century. From the early, impression-
istic approach, dialectologists switched to a concentration
on exhaustiveness and precision, especially in phonetic
description which was apparent as early as the 1930s and
1940s. The phonemic and structural approach is most
clearly manifested in studies by Fedot Žylko (1955; 1966)
and Ljudmila Kalnyn (1973).
The linguistic-geographic school was most outspokenly
represented in the studies of Petro Buzuk, Vasyl S.
Vaščenko (both on the Poltava region), and Ivan Pan'kevyč
(1938, for Transcarpathia). Pan'kevyč (1938) used the
method of linguistic-geography in investigating Ukrainian
dialects of Carpathian Rus' and neighbouring lands.

---

[28] The latter is also known as 'the father of Ukrainian dialectology'.

[29] In Shevelov's words: "From her systematic study of the phonetics
of northern and southwestern Ukrainian dialects, particularly of
their accentuation, which expanded on Vsevolod Hantsov's research, Kurylo concluded that Ukrainian arose from the merging
of two originally distinct dialectal groups". Cf. http://www.ency-
clopediaofukraine.com/display.asp?linkpath=
pages%5CK%5CU%5CKuryloOlena.htm

Chapter 1

Particularly original and influential in Ukrainian dialectology was what may be called the genetic school, which combined attention to features of a given dialect, elements of linguistic geography, and the use of dialectal material in an attempt at the historical reconstruction of the origin of a given dialect and the Ukrainian language as a whole. The founders of this trend were the already mentioned Vsevolod Hancov and Olena Kurylo; they were later joined by Ivan Žilynskyj, Władysław Kuraszkiewicz, Tetjana Nazarova and others (cf. Shevelov 1984: 666-667).

1.2.1. Dialectal atlases

The problems of dialectal classification and territorial distribution created the premises for a series of geo-linguistic works.

In the early 20th century, cartography and language geography within the former Russian empire was given a strong impulse by the work of the Moscow Dialectological Commission after the publication of its *Opyt dialektologičeskoj karty russkogo jazyka v Evrope* (1915).[30]

Fundamental contributions to Ukrainian cartography in the 20th century were made by Zilyns'kyj (1916, 1933), Hancov (1924), Žylko (1955; 1966), Dzendzelivs'kyj (1958; 1960; 1993), Bevzenko (1980), Matvjas (1990), Hrycenko (1984; 1990) and others.

A series of regional Atlases began with Tarnacki. He mapped the western Pollisian lexis of 90 settlements in Ukraine, and to a lesser extent, in Belarus'. The aim of this

---

[30] This map played a significant role since it described the East Slavic language borders, such as Belarusian-Russian and Ukrainian-Belarusian, focusing on language facts rather than political-administrative criteria. The work of the commission relied on criteria formerly expressed by Karskij (1903) and Mychal'čuk (1877).

work was to show the lexical differentiation of Polissia (Tarnacki 1939: 72-78).[31]
Among other important regional Atlases issued after the Second World War, one can mention the *Atlas of the Ternopil' Region by* Dejny (1957); Dzendzelivs'kyj's *Linguistic Atlas of Ukrainian Folk Dialects of the Transcarpathian Region of USSR (Лінгвістичний атлас українських народних говорів Закарпатської області УРСР (України): Лексика)* which was issued between 1958-1993 in three parts; Vaščenko's *Language geography of the Central Dnipro (Dnieper) Dialects (Лінгвістична географія Наддніпрянщини, 1968).*
Among dialectal atlases, which mainly had a regional character, one can mention Stieber's *Atlas językowy dawnej Lemkowszczyzny (Linguistic Atlas of the Ancient Lemko Region,* 8 issues, 1956-64), the already reported Dzendzelivs'kyj (1958-1993). The *Atlas of Ukrainian Dialects in eastern Slovakia* by Vasyl' Latta remained in manuscript as did for a long time the three-volume all-Ukrainian atlas edited by Fedot Žylko and completed by the early 1970s.[32]
Particularly numerous are the atlases devoted to the Polissian and the Carpathian areas: Kurylenko (2004), Levančēvič (1993), Nazarova (1985), Omel'kovec' (2003), Ponomar (1997), Tarnacki (1939). For the Carpathian region: Budovskaja (1992), Dzendzelivs'kyj (1958-1993), Hanudel' (1981-2010), Lyzanec' (1976), Rieger (1980–1981), *Obščekarpatskij dialektologičeskij atlas* (Bernštejn et al. 1976). The number of atlases of central and eastern dialects is more limited: Martynova 2000; 2003; Vaščenko 1962; 1968. For word-formation, see Zakrevs'ka (1976).
We schematically report in the table below some of the most well-known dialectal atlases[33]

---

[31] Also, Rieger (2014: 2077).

[32] See: http://www.inmo.org.ua/history/famous-workers/fedot-troximovich-zhilko.html.

[33] See: Prylypko (2004: 35); Hrycenko (2004: 36); Rieger (2014: 2074-2082).

Chapter 1

Table 1

UKRAINIAN DIALECTAL ATLASES		
Authors	**Atlas type**	**Published at**
Arkušyn (2008)	*Atlas myslyvs'koji leksyky Zachidnogo Polissja* (Atlas of the huntig lexis of West Polissia)	Luc'k
Arkušyn (2008)	*Atlas zachidnopolis'kych faunonomeniv* (Atlas of West Polissian Fauna Nomenclature)	Luc'k
AUM (1984 - 2001)	*Atlas ukrajins'koji movy.* Vol. 1-3. (Atlas of the Ukrainian Language)	Kyjiv
Bernštejn et al. (1967)	*Karpatskij dialektologičeskij atlas* (Carpathian Dialect Atlas)	Moskva
Čyruk (2010)	*Atlas entomolohičnoji leksyky Zachidnoho Polissja* (Atlas of the Entomological Lexis of west Polissia)	Luc'k
Czyżewski (1986)	*Atlas gwar polskich i ukraińskich okolic Włodawy* (Atlas of Polish and Ukrainian Dialects of the district of Włodawa)	Lublin
Dejna (1957)	*Gwary ukraińskie Tarnopolszczyzny* (Ukrainian Dialects in the Area of Ternopil)	Wrocław
Dzendzelivs'kyj (1958-1993)	*Linhvistyčnyj atlas Zakarpats'koji oblasti URSR (Ukrajiny): Leksyka.* Ch. 1-3 (Linguistic Atlas of the Ukrainian Folk Dialects of the Transcarpathian region of the USSR (Ukraine): Lexis. Vol 1-3)	Užhorod
Hanudel (1981-2010)	*Linhvistyčnyj atlas ukrajins'kych hovoriv schidnoji Slovaččyny.* I-IV (Linguistic Atlas of Ukranian Dialects of eastern Slovakia)	Bratislava/ Prjašiv (Prešov)
Herman (1994-1998)	*Atlas ukrajins'kych hovirok Pivničnoji Bukovyny. I. Fonetyka. Fonolohija. II. Slovozmina. Službebni slova* (Atlas of the Ukrainian Dialects of northern Bukovyna. Phonetics. Phonology. Declension)	Černivci
Hlukhovceva (2003)	*Linhvistycznyj atlas leksyky narodnoho pobutu ukrajins'kych schidnoslobožans'kych hovirok* (Linguistic Atlas of the Lexis of Everyday Life of the Ukrainian eastern Sloboda Dialects)	Luhans'k
Jevtušok (1993)	*Atlas budivel'noji leksyky zachidnoho Polissja* (Atlas of the Construction Lexis of western Polissia)	Rivne
Kurylenko (2004)	*Atlas leksyky tvarynnyctva u polis'kych dialektach* (Atlas of the Zootechnic Lexis in the Polissian Dialects)	Hlukhiv
Latta (1991)	*Atlas ukrajins'kych hovoriv schidnoji Slovaččyny* (Atlas of the Ukrainian Dialects of eastern Slovakia)	Prjašiv (Prešov)
Lyzanec' (1976)	*Atlas leksyčnych madjaryzmiv ta jich vidpovidnykiv v ukrajins'kych hovorach Zakarpats'koji oblasti URSR* (Atlas of lexical madiarisms and their equivalents in the Ukrainian dialects of the region of Transcarpathia URSR)	Užhorod

30

Martynova (2000)	*Atlas pobutovoji leksyky pravoberež- nočer- kas'kych hovirok* (Atlas of the everyday Lexis of the right-bank Čerkasy dialects)	Čerkasy
Nazarova (1985)	*Linhvistyčnyj atlas nyžn'oji Pryp'jati* (Linguistic Atlas of the lower Prypjat' river)	Kyjiv
Nykončuk (1994)	*Leksyčnyj atlas pravoberežnoho Polissja* (Lexical Atlas of right-bank Polissia)	Kyjiv -Žyto- myr
Omelkovec' (2003)	*Atlas zachidnopolis'kych nazv likarskych roslyn* (Atlas of western Polissian Denominations of Heeling Herbs)	Luc'k
Onyškevyč (un-publ.)	*Atlas of San and Lemko dialects*	Instytut Ukrajino-znavstva L'viv
Rieger (1980-1981)	*Atlas gwar bojkowskich. Opracowany głównie na podstawie zapisów S. Hrabca.* I-VII (Atlas of Bojko dialects. Elaborated on the basis of S. Hrabec's Recordings)	Wrocław
Rieger,Janów (1996)	*A Lexical Atlas of the Hutsul Dialects of the Ukrainian Language. Compiled and Edited from the Fieldnotes of Jan Janów and His Students.*	Cambridge (MA)
Sabadoš (1999)	*Atlas botaničnoji leksyky ukrajins'koji movy* (Atlas of the Botanic Lexis of the Ukrainian Language)	Užhorod
Stieber (1956-1964)	*Atlas językowy dawnej Lemkowszczyzny* (Linguistic Atlas of the former Lemko Region)	Łódź
Tarnacki (1939)	*Studia porównawcze nad geografią wyrazów (Polesie-Mazowsze)* (Comparative Studies on the Geography of Expressions of Polissia-Mazovia)	Warszawa

The most significant achievement of Ukrainian language geography and cartography is the Atlas of the Ukrainian Language (Атлас української мови), generally abbreviated as AUM (АУМ 1984-2001). The structure of this authoritative work and the way linguistic facts have been mapped give a complete picture of the dialectal differentiation within the Ukrainian language area, and its areal connections with bordering languages.

The Atlas is made up of three imposing volumes. The first one is devoted to the cartographic representation of the Polissia, Central Dnipro (Dnieper) regions and adjacent lands. This territory situated between 28 and 45° of eastern longitude extends from the boundary with Belarusian in the north-west down to the northern part of the regions of Odessa and Mykolajiv. This includes the following areas: a large, eastern part of the region of Vinnycja, Čerkasy, the western part of the Poltava region, almost all the region of

31

Kirovohrad, part of the Dnipropetrovs'k, and the western part of the region of Charkiv. In addition a small area of the adjacent region of Homel' (Belarus') and of Kursk (Russian Federation) are included.

Volume two includes the regions of Volhyn', Central Dnister area, Transcarpathia (Transcarpathian Ukraine) and neighbouring lands. It more exactly includes the regions of Rivne, Volhyn', L'viv, Ternopil', Chmel'nyc'ky, Černivec', Ivano-Frankivs'k, Transcarpathia, and the western part of Žytomyr and Vinnycja. The Ukrainian dialects spoken in neighbouring lands, such as Belarus', Poland, Slovakia, Romania and former Yugoslavia are also included in this tome.

The third volume consists of three parts. The first part covers the regions of Donec'k, Sloboda (also *Slobids'ka* or Slobožanščyna) and contiguous lands. This includes almost the entire region of Charkiv, the Donbas area, the eastern part of the Sumy, the regions of Poltava, Dnipropetrovs'k and Zaporižžja. The Ukrainian dialects spoken in the southern part of the regions of Kursk, Belgorod, Voronež and in the western part of Rostov (Russian Federation) are dealt with here.

The second part covers the "Lower Dnipro, North Black Sea areas and adjacent lands"; in details, this includes: most of the regions of Odessa and Mykolajiv, the southern part of the regions of Kirovohrad and Dnipropetrovs'k, the western part of the region of Zaporižžja, the entire region of Cherson and Crimea. The Ukrainian dialects spoken in the area of Krasnodar (Russian Federation) and in the Republic of Moldova are also assigned to this section.

Finally, the third part of the volume presents comprehensive maps of the areas described in the volumes, showing the whole Ukrainian language territory. At the end of each

volume maps with isoglosses can be viewed. The AUM covers 2359 settlements.

Map 3: Dialectal areas according to AUM[34]

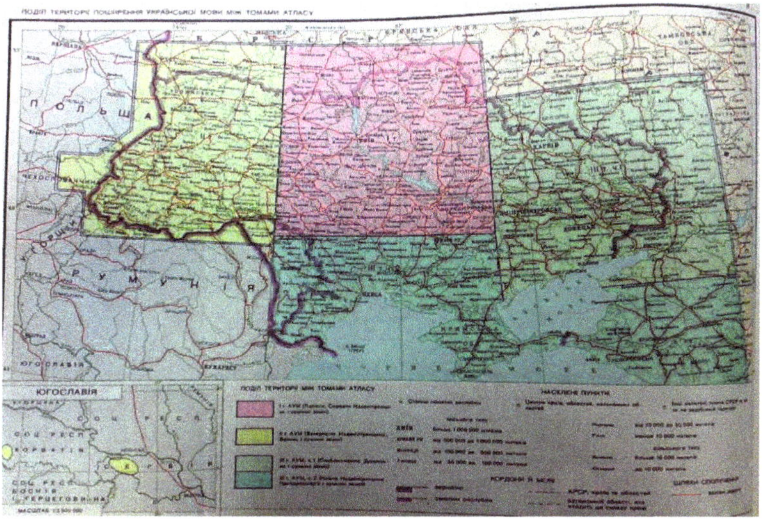

1.2.2. Dialectal dictionaries

Apart from a number of dialectal dictionaries typical of the
Soviet period, the quantity of lexicographic works has increased since 1991. In the table below a list of the most
popular dictionaries is reported:

---

[34] https://upload.wikimedia.org/wikipedia/commons/a/a0/Поділ_
території_поширення_української_мови_між_томами_атласу.jpg

Chapter 1

Table 2

DIALECTAL DICTIONARIES[35]		
Arkušyn (2000)	*Slovnyk zachidnopolis'kych hovirok* (Dictionary of west Polissian Dialects)[36]	Luc'k
Brylyns'kyj (1991)	*Slovnyk podil'skych hovoriv* (Dictionary of Podil Dialects)	Chmel'nyc'kyj
Duda (2011)	*Lemkivs'kyj slovnyk* (Lemko Dictionary)	Ternopil'
Huzar et al. (1997)	*Hucul's'ki hovirky: korotkyj slovnyk* (Hucul Dialects: a short Dictionary)	L'viv
Korzonyuk (1987)	*Матеріали до словника західноволинських говіров* (Materials for a Dictionary of west Volhyn Dialects)	Kyjiv
Lysenko (1974)	*Slovnyk polis'kych hovoriv* (Dictionary of Polissian Dialects)	Kyjiv
Matijiv (2013)	*Slovnyk hovirok central'noji Bojkivščyny* (Dictionary of the Central Bojko Dialects)	Kyjiv -Simferopol'
Moskalenko (1958)	*Slovnyk dialektyzmiv ukrajins'kych hovirok Odes'koji oblasti* (Dictionary of Dialectisms of the Ukrainian local Dialects in the Region of Odesa)	Odesa
Onyškevyč (1984)	*Slovnyk bojkivs'kych hovirok* (Dictionary of Bojko Dialects)	Kyjiv
Saharovs'kyj (2006-2007)	*Dialektnyj slovnyk Central'noji Slobožanščyny (Charkivščyny), T. 1-2)* (Dialectal Dictionary of the Central Sloboda (Charkiv) Region. Vol. 1-2)	Charkiv
Saharovs'kyj (2011)	*Materialy do dialektnoho slovnyka Central'noji Slobožanščyny* (Materials for a Dialect Dictionary of the Central Sloboda (Charkiv) Region)	Charkiv
Stupins'ka, Bytkivs'ka (2013)	*Frazeolohičnyj slovnyk lemkivs'kych hovirok* (Phraseological Dictionary of Lemko local Dialects)	Ternopil'
Šylo (2008)	*Naddnistrjans'kyj rehional'nyj slovnyk* (Regional Dictionary of the Upper Dnister Dialect)	L'viv
Tkačenko (1998)	*Kubanskij govor. Opyt avtorskogo slovarja* (Kuban dialect. Experiment of an author's dictionary)	Moskva
Tolstoj, red. (1968)	*Leksika Poles'ja: Materialy dlja polesskogo dialektnogo slovarja* (Polissian Lexis: Materials for the Polissian Dialectal Dictionary)	Moskva
Vaščenko (1960)	*Slovnyk poltavs'kych hovoriv* (Dictionary of Poltava Dialects)	Charkiv
Verchrats'kyj (1902)	*Pro hovor halyckych lemkiv* (On the Dialect of Galician Lemko)	L'viv

---

[35] For further details, see: Hrycenko (2004: 150-151); http://www.inmo.org.ua/library.html

[36] An English translation of the titles is provided in parentheses.

1.2.3. Handbooks on Ukrainian dialects

Notwithstanding a large number of dialectal studies in Ukraine, the majority of publications on various aspects of Ukrainian dialects have to be searched for in specialized journals and miscellaneous works. Significant articles, for example, were published in the nine issues of the *Dialektolohičnyj bjuleten'* (Діалектологічний бюлетень) between 1949-1962.[37] In recent years new fundamental contributions on various aspects of contemporary dialectal issues can be found in the volumes "Dialekty v sinchroniji ta diachroniji" under the redaction of Hrycenko (2014; 2015).

This situation represents a limitation for those foreign students or even scholars who just want to gain a quick overview of Ukrainian dialects.

A lack of up-to-date manuals was also lamented by Ukrainian students until relatively recent years. Since 2010 there has been a rapid increase in the publication of a whole series of textbooks, study-guides and minor manuals on Ukrainian dialectology, mainly addressed to university students and meant for didactic purposes and use in seminars. Most of these recent introductions to Ukrainian dialectology, partially replacing those classic manuals, published in the Soviet period, do not substantially provide new factual material.

The most used traditional books on Ukrainian dialectology are in increasing order of difficulty: Bevzenko (1980); Žylko (1955; 1966) and Matvijas (1990). It should however be pointed out that they were addressed to different readerships and written in different periods.

---

[37] For further details, see:
http://litopys.org.ua/ukrmova/um157.htm;
http://www1.nas.gov.ua/institutes/ium/Structure/Departments/Department4/Pages/dial_period.aspx

Žylko's works are generally considered a compromise between a monograph and a handbook on Ukrainian dialectology. Žylko is usually recommended also by dialectologists of the Institute of Ukrainian Language of the Ukrainian Academy of Sciences as a main reference on Ukrainian dialectology. This book probably represents the most valid account of different aspects of Ukrainian dialectology and is illustrated with several maps which were particularly useful in the decades preceding the publication of the Atlas of the Ukrainian Language (AUM). Nevertheless Žylko's description, may not always be suitable for the practical purposes of Ukrainian students-beginners, and even less so for a foreign student approaching Ukrainian dialectology for the first time.

Matvijas' monograph "Ukrajins'ka mova i jiji hovory" (1990) is probably the most recent broad overview of Ukrainian dialects.

Bevzenko's "Dialektolohija" (1980), probably, still remains the best preliminary insight into Ukrainian diatopic variation: it clearly summarizes the main features of Ukrainian dialects in an accessible way. For this reason, it is still widely used in University courses despite the increased number of contemporary textbooks and manuals.

Additional short accounts on Ukrainian dialectology are Hrycenko's contributions in the latest editions of "The Encyclopaedia of Ukrainian" (Hrycenko 2004: 146-151; 2007: 154-156).

Apart from the above-mentioned books whose approach is theoretical-practical, a few more manuals meant for classroom work are listed in the following table:

Table 3

HANDBOOKS FOR PRACTICAL SEMINARS		
AUTHORS	**TITLE**[38]	**DESCRIPTION**
Moskalenko (1965-66)	*Materialiv dlja praktyčnych zanjat' z ukrajins'koji dialektolohiji z metodyčnymy rekomendacijamy* (Materials for Practical Classes on the Ukrainian Dialectology with methodological references)	The book supplies dialectal texts from the region of Odesa.
Bevzenko (1970)	*Praktyčni zanjattja z ukrajins'koji dialektolohiji* (Practical Classes on Ukrainian dialectology)	The textbook provides a large number of exercises drawn from dialectal texts and questions covering main dialectal topics.
Mohyla (1974)	*Ukrajins'ka dialektolohija* (Ukrainian Dialectology)	The book provides substantial theoretical material and tests for the student. The practical part relies heavily on Bevzenko's work.
Bevzenko (1977)	*Hovory ukrajins'koji movy* (Dialects of the Ukrainian Language)	This textbook was a significant step forward for practical use by students. It is still widely used for didactic purposes.
Bevzenko (1987)	*Ukrajins'ka dialektolohija: zbirnyk prav i zavdan'* (Ukrainian Dialectology: collection of excercizes)	This textbook covers all the theoretical aspects covered in the manual issued by the same author in 1980.
Hlibčuk (2000)	*Praktyčni zavdannja z ukrajins'koji dialektolohiji* (Practical Assignments on the Ukrainian Dialectology)	The textbook contains a number of exercises covering all main aspects of Ukrainian dialectology: phonetic, morphological and lexical. Moreover, the book is complemented with a glossary of dialectal terminology.
Serdeha & Saharovs'kyj (2011)	*Ukrajins'ka dialektolohija* (Ukrainian Dialectology)	The textbook compactly provides an overview of previous works on Ukrainian dialectology. It combines theoretical and practical parts. It is orientated to the elementary needs of classroom work. Main aspects of dialectal grammar are dealt with. A large number of exercises and references complements this practical approach to the study of Ukrainian dialects.

---

[38] The list of textbooks reported is not exhaustive. There are many other contributions which could have been added, but the list has mainly an illustrative purpose.

Outside Ukraine, among surveys on Ukrainian dialects Shevelov's contributions should be mentioned. Ample space is dedicated to some historical aspects of Ukrainian dialects in his seminal work a "Historical phonology of the Ukrainian language" (1979: 35-40). Short classifications and accounts of their idiosyncratic features can be consulted in the Encyclopedia of Ukraine (Shevelov 1984: 666-667), and in the chapter devoted to "Ukrainian" in the volume "Slavonic Languages" edited by Comrie and Greville (Shevelov 1993: 993-996). Some of the most representative features of Ukrainian dialects are concisely reported in the volume "The Slavic Languages" (Sussex & Cubberley 2006: 517-521).

In the German speaking countries a few short descriptions of Ukrainian dialects[39] can be consulted in the third volume of Sociolinguistics/Soziolinguistik by Ammon et al. (2006: 1861). A very few lines on Ukrainian dialects can be found in the "Einführung in die Slavischen Sprachen" (Schweier 2012: 106-108).

In the voluminous and comprehensive second volume "Die slavischen Sprachen. Ein internationaler Handbuch zu ihren Strukturen, ihrer Geschichte und ihrer Erforschung" edited by Kempgen et al. (2014), explicit contributions on Ukrainian dialects are absent. The only exception is represented by Rieger's contribution in which the author proposes a survey on Ukrainian dialectal Atlases within the context of East Slavic dialectal Atlases (Rieger 2014: 2074-2082).

Finally, it is worth underlining that the main phonetic features (without experimental data) are traditionally well outlined in Ukrainian handbooks. Lexis and phraseology are also well illustrated. Studies on derivation and morpho-syntax are generally more limited.

---

[39] Articles on Ukrainian dialects can be found in Horbatsch (1987).

1.3. Conceptual-terminological peculiarities of Ukrainian dialectology

The structural approach to the study of Ukrainian dialects, distinctive of the first half of the 20th century, reached its full expression in the 1960s.[40] It is characterized by a series of conceptual differentiations which are somewhat extraneous to the west European and English dialectological traditions.

The term "dialect", as mentioned in the introductory section, implies a series of debatable issues. Its definition is even more complex in East Slavic dialectology, and particularly in Ukrainian. In these languages, in fact, it functions as a kind of hyperonym to which minor dialectal units are hierarchically subordinated. Many of these conceptual units remain misleading for the majority of readers approaching Ukrainian dialectology for the first time. Therefore some basic terms of Ukrainian dialectology will be introduced and discussed.[41] All other classificatory concepts, particularly those which are less frequent today, will be reported in the glossary at the end of the book. Familiarity with the Ukrainian dialectal terminology will be a useful interpretational key to easily access Ukrainian dialectal works.

Ukrainian dialectology distinguishes between at least three main, and some minor, conceptual terms:

---

[40] This coincides with the period when Žylko published the last of his three monographs dedicated to Ukrainian dialectology (1966).

[41] The content of the section largely relies on a previous paper. Cf. Del Gaudio (2015: 11-15).

Table 4

UKRAINIAN DIALECTAL UNITS	
hovirka (говірка)	smaller dialectal unit; e.g. a dialect as spoken in a single place.
dialect or hovir (діалект - говір)	generic term to mean either a single, local dialect or the dialectal variety of a localized area.
pidnaríččja (піднаріччя)	slightly smaller unit than the *naríččja*.
naríččja (наріччя)	largest grouping of dialects.

If we compare some fundamental definitions of dialectal units in Ukrainian:

1) *The language of one or more inhabited centres/communities is called* **hovirka**. *A group of related hovirky, sharing common features, forms a* **hovir**. *Hovory (hovors) which share common features belong to particular group of hovory. Large dialectal groupings of the language, to which different hovory (***dialects)*** belong and which are shaped by common phonetic, grammatical and lexical features are called* **dialectal groups**. *Moreover, the scholarly literature also uses the term* **naríččja**, *with which refers to a* **larger dialectal grouping**. *Another well-known term is* **pidnaríččja** *used in reference to a smaller dialectal group than that covered by the term* **naríččja**. *[...] The term* **dialect** *is mainly used as a synonym for the term "hovir", and sometimes also as a synonym of a group of hovors. At the same time the term* **dialect** *may sometimes be used as a general, familiar concept indicating different territorial varieties of the language (hovirka, hovir, naríččja and pidnaríččja) differing one from another to a certain extent*[42] (Cf. Žylko 1955: 3-4).

---

[42] *Мова одного або кількох населених пунктів називається* **говіркою**. *Група споріднених говірок, що мають спільні риси, утворює* **говір**. *Говори, що мають спільні риси, входять до певної групи говорів. Широкі діалектні угрупування мови народу, до складу яких входять, як правило, різні говори (діа-*

2) *A group of uniform **hovirky**, related to one another by a series of specific language features, differentiating them, more or less clearly, from other groups of hovirky, is called **hovir**.*
*A **hovir** is a territorially delimited dialectal formation characterized by a certain number of dialectal features. On a dialectal map hovory are delimited one from another by a bunch of isoglosses which intensify in the border areas. In the meaning of **hovir** one also uses the term **dialect**, although the latter also designates a group of related hovory, characterized by a system of common features, clearly differentiating this group from another group of hovory[43]* [Cf. Bevzenko 1980: 6].
3) *The Ukrainian dialectal language is made up of larger and smaller units, each of which appears on a specific, delimited territory. The smallest territorial dialectal*

---

*лекти), що об'єднуються спільними фонетичними, граматичними і лексичними рисами, звуться **діалектними групами**. Крім того, в науці вживаний ще термін **наріччя**, під яким розуміється найширше **діалектне угрупування**. Відомий також і термін **піднаріччя**, для позначення вужчого, ніж наріччя, діалектного угрупування. […] Термін **діалект** здебільшого вживається як синонім слова «говір», а іноді – як **група говорів**. Поряд з цим термін **діалект** часом застосовується як загальне, родове поняття, що позначає різні територіальні відміни загальнонародної мови (говірка, говір, наріччя і піднаріччя), які різняться між собою певним обсягом.*

[43] *Групу однотипних говірок, що споріднені між собою рядом специфічних мовних ознак, якими вони більш-менш відчутно відрізняються від інших груп говірок, звуть **говором**. Говір — це територіально окреслене діалектне утворення, яке характеризується певною сукупністю діалектних ознак. На діалектологічній карті говори відмежовуються один від одного пасмом ізоглос, що скупчуються на пограниччях говорів. У значенні **говір** вживають і термін **діалект**, хоч останнім позначають також групу споріднених говорів, що характеризуються системою спільних ознак, якими ця група виразно відрізняється від іншої групи говорів.*

41

unit is **hovirka**. *[...] The hovirka covers one or more inhabited centres. The hovirky are differentiated one from another by a minimal number of dialectal traits. The hovirky are delimited not on the basis of the language features characterizing them but on the number of traits forming a microsystem. A group of related hovirky forms a larger territorial unit called* **hovir** *or* **dialect**. *Hovory are differentiated on the basis of a relatively larger number of phonetic, grammatical and lexical dialectal features. The totality of related hovory or dialects forms the largest dialectal, territorial unit, i.e.,* **naričča**[44] (Matvijas 1990: 9).

The clearest explanation for the western European reader appears to be that of Žylko. He specified that the word *dialect* in colloquial usage is a kind of 'hyperonym', covering all types of dialectal units and subunits, e.g. *pidnaričča*; in this respect the term has a similar use to the western European dialectlogical tradition. Furthermore, on the basis of the compared citations, one needs to point out that

- the **hovirka** (*говірка*) functions as a real communicative system[45]. In other words, it is the minimal territorial, structured dialectal unit which includes the

---

[44] *Українська діалектна мова складається з більших і менших одиниць, кожна з яких виступає на певній обмеженій території. Найменшою територіальною діалектною одиницею є* **говірка**. *[...] Говірка охоплює один або (рідше) кілька населених пунктів. Говірки розрізняються між собою певною незначною кількістю діалектних явищ. Виділяються говірки не за наявністю мовних рис, характерних тільки для них, а за сукупністю явищ, які об'єднуються в певну мікросистему. Група споріднених говірок об'єднується в більшу територіальну одиницю —* **говір** *або* **діалект**. *Говори розрізняються порівняно великою кількістю фонетичних, граматичних і лексичних діалектних рис. Сукупність споріднених говорів або діалектів утворює найбільшу діалектну територіальну одиницю —* **наріччя**.

[45] *Говірка — найменша одиниця територіальної диференціації діалектичної мови. У структурі мовно-територіальних утворень (говірка — говір/діалект — наріччя) лише говірка є*

language of one and, sometimes, more inhabited localities, on whose territory there is no significant variation. A group of related minimal dialectal units, i.e. *hovirky,* sharing similar characteristics but slightly differing from other groups of *hovirky,* form the *hovory.*

- A *hovir* or *dialect* can be therefore defined as a territorially well delineated, major dialectal unit unifying a group of smaller units (*hovirky*). It is characterized by a specific number of similar dialectal features, e.g. phonetic, accentuation, grammatical, lexical, phraselogical etc. On a dialectal map, these larger dialectal units (*hovory*) are delimited by a belt of isoglosses which tend to intensify in the area where they border other dialectal groups [Bevzenko 1980: 6]. The term *dialect* can be used as a synonym of *hovir*. Nevertheless, this word may also designate a group of kindred *hovory* characterized by a system of common features, differentiating them from another group.
- In other words, *dialect*, in Ukrainian dialectology, besides being used as a synonym for "*hovir*", may also indicate, as a kind of 'hyperonym', the largest dialectal unit in the subdivision of the language territory in vast dialectal areas, e.g. *the northern dialects*, the *south-western dialects* etc. In this sense, however, Ukrainian dialectology tends to use the term *"naríččja"* (*наріччя*). This covers an entire group of dialects on a large territorial scale, showing a series of common linguistic features distinct from the general characteristics of another dialectal group or *naríččja*. Thus the *naríččja* roughly corresponds to the largest dialectal partition or dialectal group (main vernacu-

---

реальною комунікаційною системою, засобом спілкування мешканців одного, рідше кількох населених пунктів, принципово рівнозначною мові. Cf. Hrycenko (2004: 102).

lar; a sort of a generalized dialectal-territorial variation), e.g. the Polissian dialectal group or northern dialects etc.

- A slightly smaller unit that the *naričča* and subordinated to the latter is the *pidnaričča.*

The specificity of Ukrainian terminology can be conceptually expressed in English only with a certain degree of approximation. Therefore, the term **hovirka** can be approximately rendered in English as a 'local dialect' of a single (distinct) inhabited community. *Naričča* would be the equivalent of a larger territorial group of dialects, and *pidnaričča* is a subgroup of the latter. The English word *dialect* has evidently a larger semantic field, covering both the Ukrainian concepts of *"hovory"* and *"hovirky"*, even though for the latter the word *patois*[46] or local dialect (cf. Ukr. *misceva hovirka*) may sometimes be used.

Finally, other important operational concepts are those of **convergence or integration** involving linguistic, dialectal unification → process of homogenization and **divergence or differentiation** involving differentiation → heterogenisation. The further terminological differentiation of dialectal elements in: dialectal feature (cf. діалектна риса) vs. dialectal structure and microsystems (cf. діалектна структура та микросистеми) will be not dealt with here.

1.4. Research aims and utility of Ukrainian dialectology

Ukrainian dialectology studies the functioning of the vernacular language (cf. *žyva narodna mova*/жива народна мова) in all its diversification and variation. It examines the geographic diffusion of dialectal phenomena, it separates and delineates particular dialectal facts within the dialectal system. In simple words, Ukrainian dialectology describes territorial dialects (diatopic variation).

---

[46] This term derives from French dialectology.

Chapter 1

In Ukrainian dialectology one can observe a clear separation between a social dialectology (sociolinguistics) which studies speech variation of particular social and professional groups, mainly within an urban environment and dialectology.[47]

The Ukrainian tradition also differentiates between a descriptive and historical dialectology. The former adopts a synchronic and statistic approach; the latter investigates dialects in their diachronic dimension.

In primary and secondary education, the knowledge of the dialect spoken in a particular district is an essential condition to individuate and avoid possible sources of interference, thus enhancing the level of standard Ukrainian.

Dialectology and its data are particularly useful for a more accurate interpretation of historical documents and for a more reliable reconstruction of earlier developmental stages of Ukrainian (as with any other language). Local dialects often preserve language relicts of earlier phases which may not come up in historical documents and whose traces are apparently lost. There are cases, therefore, where only dialectal data can shed light on and account for the sudden occurrence of specific language elements in classical as well as in contemporary works of Ukrainian literature. A preliminary knowledge of dialectal facts helps to overcome some comprehension difficulties of certain texts. This aspect links dialectology to literary studies, in particular to text analysis and stylistics. Many are the writers of the 19th and early 20th centuries who made use of dialectal elements in their works. From the point of view of the contemporary speaker they turned to dialectisms in order to achieve special stylistic effects (e.g. typification of certain characters) or to render aspects of

---

[47] We shall return to this point in section 3.3.

geo-linguistic landscape and local culture.[48] This statement is only partially true since most 19th century writers used their regional language because there was no complete consensus on which dialect to base a new standard (cf. Danylenko 2015). For example, Bukovinian dialectisms are found in Fed'kovyč and Kobyljans'ka; Podillian elements in Svydnyc'kyj; Franko used elements from the Bojko dialects; Lesja Ukrajinka and Hlibov recurred to Polissian; Čeremšyn to the Huculian; Slobodian elements are typical of Kvitka-Osnov"janenko.

In addition, modern Ukrainian, in the period of its formation and standardization (19th century, first two decades of the 20th century) did not display a unified norm in grammar and lexical choice. Dialectal differentiation played an important role. Certain textual and author's idiosyncrasies (morphology, syntax, lexis, phraseology), especially in writers of the 19th century such as Kotljarevs'kyj, Kvitka-Osnov"janenko, Ševčenko and others, can be regarded from the point of view of the contemporary Ukrainian standard norm as dialectal or, as some Ukrainian sociolinguists say "suržyk".[49]

Moreover, dialectal factual materials, besides their linguistic interest, are also important for related disciplines such as history, archaeology, ethnography, and cultural studies in general.

1.5. Research methods in Ukrainian dialectology

The most widely applied approach used in Ukrainian dialectology to study and gather dialectal material consists in

---

[48] Contemporary writers may also use elements of Ukrainian-Russian mixed speech ("suržyk") to reach certain stylistic devices. See: chapter 3.

[49] Cf. section 3.1.

the direct observation of the oral language of dialect speakers and its notation. This task is generally carried out by an expert with a linguistic/dialectological background.

In the case of a dialectological expedition, participants attentively listen to the local dialect and identify (elicit) its characteristic features. At the same time, they study the social composition of the indigenous population and geohistorical background of the settlement.

Dialectologists usually get in touch with the local institutions, for example the director of the local school and the local council. The selection of informants - a fundamental step in any research on language variation - is often carried out thanks to the help of local teachers and employees. Informants have to be, as a rule, at least third generation natives of the village who were not particularly mobile and who did not move to another place for long periods of time. Their speech has to be recognized as typical of that particular community.

In a strict dialectal approach to language facts, one certainly needs to consider the interaction between standard language(s) and dialects. Many dialectal features tend to disappear in time under the influence of the standard or may be subject to modifications.

The selection of the most representative speakers of a specific dialect is traditionally considered to be an essential step for a successful outcome of a dialectal expedition. As a rule in (East Slavic) dialectology, the individuation of those locals whose speech reflects the most archetypal features of a given dialect remains a fundamental postulate.[50]

---

[50] Žylko wrote to this purpose: "Для запису діалектних матеріалів важливо дібрати саме такі об'єкти, щоб мова їх була найбільш типовою для певної говірки або діалекту [...]. Добирати об'єкти для запису треба, як уже зазначалось, з типовою для даного населеного пункту мовою. [...] Як правило, старі люди більше зберігають давніші елементи говору (діалекту)". Translation: "For the recording of dialectal materials it is important to exactly select those informants whose language is the most typical of a specific dialect [...] One should

Traditional field techniques of a dialectal survey can be schematized in the following points:

- language material has to be recorded from native inhabitants who have always lived there and speak the local dialect;
- informants have to belong to different age groups and one needs to differentiate between:
  a) speakers of the older generation who preserve in their speech old and archaic features;
  b) speakers of the middle generation (35-50);
  c) young generation, for example school children, students etc.
- transcribe / make a note of lexical items and language forms within the context of a sentence. A rare word (from sayings, proverbs, tales and similar) has to be accompanied by an appropriate comment.
- In case of doubt about a particular form, it is necessary to ask and check with other informants. If it is still unclear a commentary is appropriate.
- If a lexical item, a particular construction, has disappeared from the local speech, one needs to ask older people about its usage and when, if possible, it died out.
- Dialectal material is usually transcribed in a simplified phonetic (phonemic) transcription. Accent is indicated on each word, except for monosyllabic ones. Much emphasis is also given to the authenticity of the collected data, their systematization and the exactness of their transcription.

Today dialectology also makes use of technical aids, such as tape-recorders, video and other devices, since they allow the observation and analysis of speech fragments in their functional context.

---

choose those objects for the recording, as already mentioned, which show the typical way of speaking of a particular settlement. [...] As a rule old people better preserve the older elements of a given dialect" (Žylko 1966: 273-275).

1.6. Transcription of Ukrainian dialects

Transcription is a system of symbols used for the written representation of oral speech. Transcription can be defined as a special notation system of oral speech which adopts a series of symbols based on the contemporary Ukrainian alphabet with the addition of specific graphemes (letters) from other alphabets, mostly from the Latin alphabet, and diacritics (diacritical signs).

There are various types of transcription based on different principles. The two main principles are:
1) the phonetic and
2) the phonematic transcriptions.

Phonetic transcription (also phonetic script or phonetic notation) is the visual representation of speech sounds (or phones). The most common type of phonetic transcription uses a phonetic alphabet, such as the International Phonetic Alphabet (IPA or API). This notation system tries to reproduce the phonetic characteristics of spoken language with a high degree of exactness.

A notation system that only reports the phonemes of a certain language without considering all its phonetic characteristics is called phonematic/phonemic transcription.

In the Ukrainian dialectal practice one can find both kinds of transcriptions depending on the aim of the researcher. The Ukrainian dialectal transcription is based on the Ukrainian alphabet. An exception to this generally accepted tradition, is a series of works describing south-western dialects which used a transcription based on the Latin alphabet.

The phonetic transcription can show a different level of exactness. It can be detailed or simplified (broad transcription). In the first instance there is a large use of diacritics. The latter, instead, tries to reduce to a minimum the diacritics.

The system of Ukrainian phonetic transcription can be consulted in a few classic academic works, such as

Chapter 1

Sučasna ukrajins'ka literaturna mova. Vstup. Fonetyka
(1969: 427-431); *Sučasna ukrajins'ka literaturna mova.*
Fonetyka. Orfoepija. Hrafika. Orfohrafija (Toc'ka 1981: 34-
38); *Sučasna ukrajins'ka literaturna mova. Fonetyka.*
Fonolohija. Orfoepija. Hrafika. Orfohrafija. Leksykolohija.
Leksikohrafija (Bondar et al. 2006: 42-45). On the other
hand, systematization and samples of a dialectal phonematic transcription is reported in the introductory section
of the AUM (1984), and in the classical books on Ukrainian
dialectology (cf. Žylko 1955: 19-27; Žylko 1966: 214;
Hovirky Čornobyl's'koji zony. Teksty 1996).
In the Ukrainian dialectal transcription, besides the usual
letters of Ukrainian alphabet (widely considered a phonemic alphabet): **а, б, в, г, ґ, д, е, ж, з, и, і, й, к, л, м, н, о,**
п, р, с, т, у, ф, х, ц, ч, ш additional symbols are also
used.
The basic vowels are graphemically reported as they ap-
pear in the alphabet: **а** [a], **е** [ɛ], **і** [i], **и** [ɪ], **о** [ɔ], **у** [u].
Whereas their corresponding soft-variants: **я** [ja], **ю** [ju],
є [jɛ], **ї** [ji] are transcribed as *ŭa, ŭy, ŭe, ŭi* if they convey
two phones (sounds); otherwise they are transcribed as
я → а, ю → у, є → е, when they follow a palatalized consonant; for example: *пісня* transcribed as *n'існ'а.*
Diphthongs, although untypical for standard Ukrainian,
may occur in a few dialects, particularly in the northern or
Polissian group. They can be schematically rendered in the
following way:

Table 5

Diphthongs	Transcription	Examples[51]
[ie]	*ie*	*n'іеч, хл'іеб, л'іето*
[wɔ]	*ɥo*	*куон', ɤуост*
[wɛ]	*ɥe*	*куен'*

---

[51] Due to technical difficulties, we could not represent the exact
symbols (ligature under the given examples).

50

The first type of diphthong occurs in certain positions as reflexes of former [ě] <ѣ>. There are many more reflexes than those represented in the table above as reflexes of former [e, ě, o]. We have just mentioned the most typical ones.

If the diphthong is rising (Ukr. *висхідний*), it is usually marked by an accent on the second element; on the other hand, if it is descendent (Ukr. *спадний/низхідний*) on the first one (cf. Žylko 1955: 21).

As to other vocalic symbols:

- ы stands for non-labial high central vowel [i][52] (cf. Russian), and it is typical of the Carpathian group of dialects, for example: *rukŷ* (*рукы*), *nohŷ* (*ногы*); *chytryj* (*хытрый*), *syn* (*сын*), *dym* (*дым*).
- ô – closed [o] which mainly occur in some Carpathian dialects: *kôrôvu* (*кôрôву;* cow-acc.), *côl'i* (*сôл'i*), *bôrôn'im'i* (*бôрôн'iм'i*), *pôzum* (*рôзум*), *tômu* (*тôму*) etc.
- ÿ – high front labialized/rounded vowel[53]: *nÿn* (*пÿn*), *snÿp* (*снÿп*), *vÿl* (*вÿл*), *düm* (*дÿм*), *porüg* (*порÿг*), *stül* (*стÿл*), *korüv* (*корÿв*), *domüÿ* (*домÿÿ*) etc.

A few diacritics are traditionally used in Ukrainian dialectology. The most common in vocalism are: (^) designating a closed vowel, e.g. ô; a dash sign (–) or, alternatively, two graphemes (letters): *oo* indicate a long vowel; a breve diacritic on top of the vowel shows a non-syllabic vowel; the vowel stress is marked by an acute accent ('), whereas the tonic syllable is marked by a raised vertical line (') usually preceding the accented syllable, for example: *'mucha* (*'муха*), *'bat'ko* (*'bat'ko*) Cf. AUM (1984: 10).

The transcription of consonants, by and large, follows the Ukrainian alphabet. Peculiarities, such as palatalization

---

[52] This should not be confused with the standard Ukrainian phoneme /i/ <и> which is a high-mid front vowel. In narrow IPA transcription: [ɪ].

[53] The realization of this phoneme is similar to that of German and French /ÿ:/ <ü>.

(soft consonant), its absence (hard consonant) or the softening of a consonant are marked by a few diacritics. A palatal consonant (палатальність) is marked by a (ʼ)[54]; the softening by (ˈ).

In addition, a few combinations of letters through the use of a ligature is meant to reproduce some phonetic characteristics, for example the affricates: /dʒ/ (дж̂), /ts͡/ (ц) and similar.

- A small letter used on top of the consonant may show either the sonorization of a voiceless consonant or, alternatively, its devoicing:

- $n^б$, $c^з$, $m^д$, $ш^ж$, for example: *молот^{д}ˈба* (threshing), *прос^{ь}ˈба* (request, solicitation), *ос^{ь}ˈде* (here is, there is).

- $б^п$, $д^т$, $з^с$, $ж^ш$, for example: *дуб^п* (oak), *мороз^с* (frost), *сад^т* (garden).

A more detailed description of phonematic (phonemic) transcription used in Ukrainian dialectology can be consulted in the: Atlas of the Ukrainian Language (AUM 1984: 9-10); Žylko (1955: 19-27; 1966: 28-33); Bevzenko (1980: 21-24); Dzendzelivsʼkyj (1987: 10-11) etc. Since dialects may also display a different phonemic inventory than standard Ukrainian, besides the basic guidelines reported above, a researcher may develop his/her own transcriptional system or adapt to his/her own needs some of the symbols and diacritics already illustrated. In the transcriptions of western Ukrainian dialects, for example, a Romanized alphabet has often been used.

---

[54] In some manuals and transcriptions one can also see the following diacritic (ʼ). For technical reasons we have mainly adopted the latter symbol in our examples. For details, see: AUM 1 (1984: 10).

CHAPTER 2

2. A classification of Ukrainian dialects

2.1. A historic outline

It is widely agreed that the Ukrainian dialectal territory distinguishes three major territorial-dialectal macro-areas (see Section 2.2.)
Historically Ukrainian dialects have not always been characterized by this tripartite division. At the time of ancient Rus', the population who lived on the territories which are now part of contemporary Ukraine formed two ethnolinguistic groups, one to the south-east, one to the south-west. The differentiation between these two dialect areas probably reflected the tribal division of the south-eastern Slavic tribes.
The union of different tribal groups was characterized by specific language features, and each tribe spoke its own dialect.
There are historical linguistic reasons for assuming that the ancient east Slavic vernaculars were related to those of the tribes of Poljans, D(e)revljans, Severjans and northern Volhynians; whereas the south-western dialects were related to the dialects spoken by the southern Volhynians, Uliči, Tiverci and White Croatians.[55]
Mychal'čuk associated the ancient north-eastern dialects with the vernacular spoken by the Poljans and

---

[55] As mentioned in the introduction we have tried to anglicize some of the most common ethnonyms to facilitate reading. These tribes are also known as Poljane, Derevljane, Dregoviči, Dulěbi, Severjane, Volynjane, Uliči, Tiverci etc. Cf. Shevelov (1979).

D(e)revljans. While Sěverjans and Dregovičians belonged to a transitional type between south Rusian and north Rusian tribes. Within the south-western group Dulěbs were placed in Volhyn', Croatians in Galicia; Uliči and Tiverci occupied Podillia and functioned as a transitional tribe between north-eastern and north-western groups.

The relationship existing between Ukrainian dialects and the language of the ancient east Slavic tribes, despite the complex historical-dialectal interaction and the appearance of later dialectal features, is traditionally accepted in Ukrainian dialectology. The fact that the original southern borders of the northern dialects reached farther South than today, is historically well illustrated by the initial subdivision of the principalities of Kyjiv, Perejaslav and Černihiv, core of the ancient Rus' (see Shevelov 1979: 206-212).

The postulate that contemporary south-western and south-eastern dialectal groups originally formed a larger dialectal entity (naričča) is proved by the fact that many typical features characterizing the northern dialects can be clearly opposed to the features of both southern groups (Matvijas 1990: 32).

Northern and south-western dialects are historically related. All northern dialects, and the majority of south-western ones, are more archaic if compared with the south-eastern group of relatively newer formation.[56] Both groups are characterized by varying degrees of dialectal differentiation caused by different factors:

   a) The reflection, to a certain extent, of the language spoken by the ancient tribal settlements;
   b) The historical stability of the former feudal and state-administrative borders;
   c) Moderate migration waves towards these territories (ibid.).

---

[56] In simple words, there were two main dialectal areas: the northern one and the southwestern one; the south-eastern part is a result of the colonization in the 17th -18th centuries.

Chapter 2

Although the interaction between the south-western and south-eastern groups played a major role in the stabilization of modern Ukrainian, especially from the second half of the 19th century, the influence of the northern dialects, particularly those used in the former Černihiv governorate, also had a fundamental role in the formation of modern Ukrainian. The northern (east Polissian) dialects, in fact, exerted a certain degree of influence on literary Ukrainian in the early phases of its development. The literary (chancery) language used in the 17th and 18th century Cossacks' State (or Hetmanate) reflected north-eastern Ukrainian dialectal features. The cultural centres of this State: Baturyn, Hlukhiv, Novhorod-Sivers'kyj, Starodub etc., were situated on the territory of these dialects. The core of these vernaculars was the region of Černihiv. Worth mentioning is the fact that the territorial extension of northern dialects, at the time of Kotljarevs'kyj, also encompassed the northern part of what is now the Poltava region. Therefore, many features of east Polissian were present in the vernacular spoken in this area. Today one can only observe transitional features converging towards these dialects (Shevelov 1966: 10).

The division into three main dialectal areas is mainly based on a totality of common features in a large dialectal entity, rather than on the differentiation of specific characteristics. The "Atlas of the Ukrainian language" shows that Ukrainian is divided into three main dialectal areas by a belt of isoglosses reflecting phonetic, grammatical and lexical phenomena.

The main criterion on which the south versus north delineation is based is the part played by the accent in the development of vocalism (Shevelov 1993: 947). In the north the most important vowel changes took place under stress, in the South they ran identically in stressed and unstressed syllables. This basic difference is supplemented by some other distinctions in phonology, morphology and lexicon.

According to Shevelov (1993: 948), the former two groups already began to take shape in prehistoric times, while the formation of the south-eastern dialects occurred in the 16th to 18th centuries. It was at that time that the present day south-eastern Ukraine, after being reclaimed from the Tatars by the Cossacks, was resettled or settled by people from south-western and northern regions. The unity of the south-eastern dialects was created by the dynamic migration processes and the mixing of population from territories of the two more archaic dialects.

2.2. The Ukrainian dialectal territory

The sum of specific dialectal features which characterize local dialectal micro-units (cf. hovirky) can be traced back to larger territorial variation. This diversification is traditionally conveyed into three major territorial-dialectal groups:

1. a South-western group;
2. a South-eastern group;
3. a Northern group.

South-eastern and south-western dialects share more common phonetic features than northern or Polissian dialects; the latter have quite a few specific features.

At morpho-syntactic and lexical levels, south-western dialects preserve a number of distinctive peculiarities showing a high degree of inner differentiation. Polissian dialects also demonstrate considerable variation.

The most homogeneous group is represented by south-eastern dialects. This group, with the exception of the Central Dnipro (Dnieper) sub-group, is of later formation than the northern and south-western dialects.

The dialects spoken in the Central Dnipro area, (*говори середньої Наддніпрянщини*), core of the south-eastern group, also because of their high degree of homogeneity, form the basis of modern literary Ukrainian. Despite their lower internal differentiation, south-eastern dialects, if compared to standard Ukrainian, still present a certain number of distinctive features.

The following map will better illustrate the widely accepted dialectal subdivision of the Ukrainian dialectal territory.

Map 4: Ukrainian dialectal territory[57]

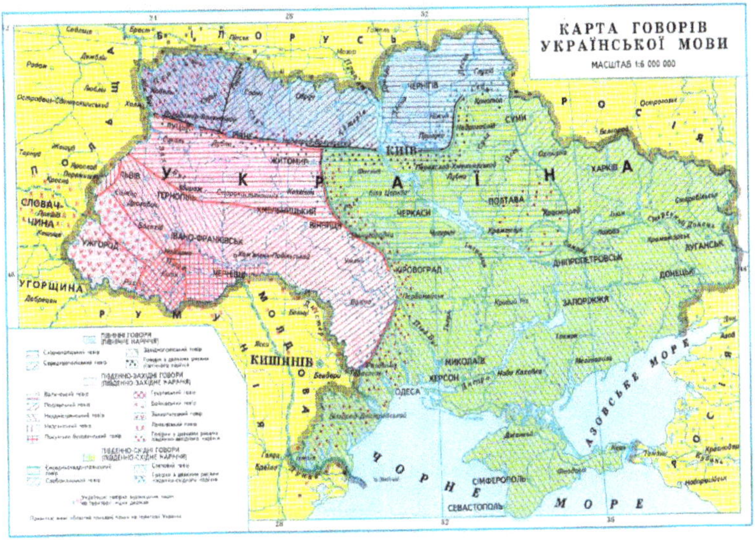

There are different classifications of Ukrainian dialects and their subgroups. Nevertheless, these taxonomies do not substantially differ one from another. The discrepancy mainly concerns the groups to be assigned to transitional areas, some dialectal subdivision (sub-groups) of south-western dialects and the spelling adopted.

In the following table we shall report Shevelov's classification of Ukrainian dialects (Shevelov 1993: 995), largely relying on Žylko (1966) and Zilyns'kyj (1979).[58]

---

[57] http://litopys.org.ua/ukrmova/um151.htm

[58] His most important work, first published in Polish in 1932, was revised and translated as *A Phonetic Description of the Ukrainian Language* in 1979. Cf. Internet Encyclopedia of Ukraine.

Table 6: A classification of Ukrainian dialect

UKRAINIAN DIALECTS		
SOUTH-EASTERN	**NORTHERN**	**SOUTH-WESTERN**
Steppe dialects	Eastern Polissian dialects	Podillja dialects
Čerkasy-Poltava dialects (Central Dnipro/Dnieper dialects)	Central Polissian dialects	South Volhynian dialects
Slobožanščyna or Sloboda dialects	Western Polissian and Pidljašian dialects	Dnister dialects
	Transitional dialects from northern and southern groups	Sjan dialects
	Transitional Ukrainian-Belarusian and Ukrainian-Russian dialects	Lemkian or Lemko dialects
		Bojkian or Bojko dialects
		Central Transcarpathian dialects
		Hucul dialects
		Pokuttia dialects
		Bukovyna dialects

http://www.encyclopediaofukraine.com/display.asp?link-path=pages%5CZ%5CI%5CZilynskyIvan.htm

Chapter 2

2.3. Dialectal macro-areas

Map 5: Subdivision of dialectal areas[59] (groups and sub-groups)

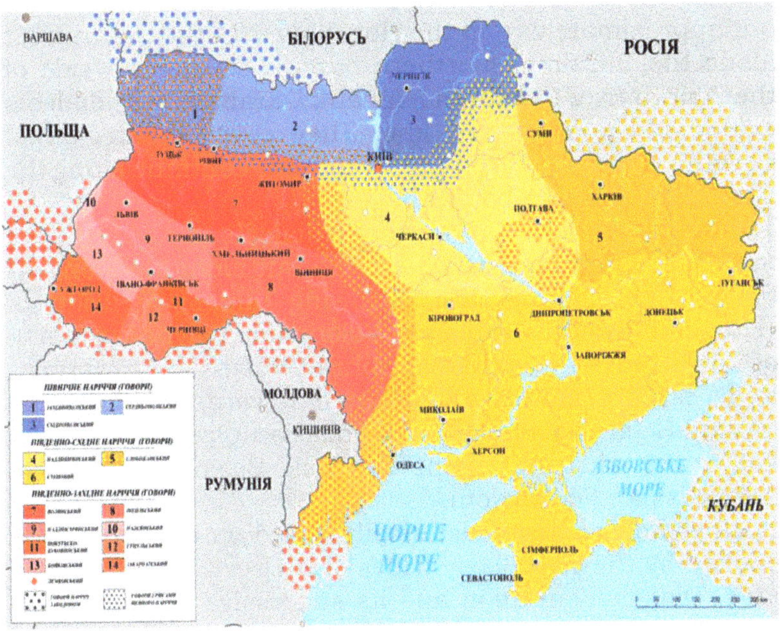

2.3.1. Northern / Polissian Ukrainian dialects

The Polissian dialectal group covers a large area in northern Ukraine. These dialects run geo-politically from the Polish border in the west through the Belarusian in the north and north-west and the Russian in the north-east. This group extends towards the Ukrainian-Belarusian transitional dialects of the Brest-Pinsk region in South-

https://commons.wikimedia.org/wiki/Category:Linguistic_maps
_of_Ukraine#/media/File:Map_of_Ukrainian_dialects.png

western Belarus'. It is separated from the south-western Belarusian dialects by a conventional line which goes from the left bank of the Narev river to the Horyn river. The western boundary is delimited by the western Buh river where the Pidljašian dialects are spoken.[60]

The northern boundary of the Polissian group stretches out approximately from the Horyn river in the South-west along the Ukrainian northern border. On the left side of the Dnipro river (northern left bank Ukraine) these dialects extend along a blurred line. They cover the region of Černihiv along the Desna river and they continue along the Ukrainian-Russian border.

The southern border of northern dialects is marked by a bundle of isoglosses which stretch out along the conventional line joining the following areas: district of *Włodawa*/Volodava (Poland), Volodymyr-Volyns'kyj (north of Luc'k), Rivne (north of Novohrad-Volyns'kyj), Žytomyr, Kyjiv, estuary/mouth of Desna river towards the rivers Oster and Sejm. Local dialects of Polissian type are also spoken in the adjacent regions of Kursk, Belgorod and Voronež (Russian Federation).

Northern dialects are historically based on the vernacular spoken by the east Slavic tribes of D(e)revlians and Sěverjans. Dialectal variation and its successive differentiation was the consequence of both intra-linguistic factors and the specific historical development of the different territories. Worth noting is that Polissian dialects share many common features with the corresponding south-western Belarusian dialects.

Most Ukrainian classifications[61] group northern dialects into four subgroups:
  1. Eastern Polissian or left bank Polissian;
  2. Central Polissian or right bank Polissian;

---

[60] Ukr. nadbuz'ko-polis'ki/pidljas'ki hovirky (надбузько-поліські/ підляські говірки).

[61] Compare: table 6.

3. Western Polissian or Volynian-Polissian;
4. Pidljašian dialects or Nadbuz'ko-Polissian.

Map 6: Approximate extension of Polissian dialects and their subdivision[62]

2.3.2. Generalized phonetic characteristics of Polissian dialects

The northern dialects, if compared with the south-western and, especially, with the south-eastern ones, are characterized by a large number of archaic features. These are particularly evident at the phonetic/phonological level. Many of its features, in fact, resemble older historical developments of Ukrainian without counterparts in modern Ukrainian literary texts.

---

[62] https://uk.wikipedia.org/wiki/%D0%9F%D0%BE%D0%BB%D1%96%D1%81%D1%81%D1%8F#/media/File:Ukraine-Polissya.png

Chapter 2

Among the phonetic features generally associated with Polissian dialects one can mention:

Vocalism

- Differentiation between accented and non-accented vocalism.
- Presence of diphthongs instead of etymological [o] in the new closed syllables with different outcomes depending on the dialectal area and the role played by the accent.
- The accented etymological [e] in newly closed syllables before hard consonants (if in the next syllable drops the weak jer [ь]) tends to develop into a diphthong. The monophthong: [i] is, however, possible. The etymological [e] however in a non-accented position keeps its value *òsen'* (*òсен*) 'autumn'.
- The outcome of former jat' [ě] in stressed position is the diphthong [ie], and in some dialectal varieties the monophthong [i]; e.g.: *d'ied* (*д'ieд*) 'grandfather', *l'ies* (*л'iec*) 'wood, forest', *b'iedny(j)* (*б'ieдни(й)*) 'poor', *na vod'ie* (*на вод'ie*) 'on-loc. the water', *na kon'ie* (*на кон'ie*) 'ahorse' etc.
- Outcome /a/ in place of historic <ę> in stressed position, for example: pjat', 'five'. In atonic position /e/.
- Akannja (non-accented [o] in the pre-tonic syllable is pronounced almost like [a]) is particularly strong in the eastern Polissian subgroup, especially in the northern ones, as we shall see later; e.g.: *karova* (*каро̀ва*) 'cow', *vada* (*вада̀*) 'water' etc. However, it is present, to a lesser extent, also in the Western and Central parts of Right Bank Polissian.

Chapter 2

Consonants

- Different distribution in the opposition of hard vs palatalized consonants, and voiced vs unvoiced consonants.
- Hardening (loss of the palatalized correlation) in most dialects of such consonants as /r'/ >/r/, cf. *burjak* (буряк) vs *burak* (бурак) 'beetroot'; *kurju* (курю) vs *kuru* (куру) 'I smoke'; *zorja* (зоря) vs *zora* (зора) 'star'. The same can be said for /c/ [ts] in specific phonic combinations: [tsa, tso, tsu] or in suffixes: -c-, -ec-, for example: *ulycja* (улиця) vs *ulica* (улица) 'street'; *chlopec'* (хлопець) vs *chlopec* (хлопец) 'boy'.
- Polissian dialects tend to keep the voiced consonants at the word and morpheme boundaries before unvoiced consonants, e.g. *horod* (город) 'town', *kazka* (казка) 'tale', *zub* (зуб) 'tooth' etc. Nevertheless voiced consonants in some parts of Right Bank Polissian dialects, particularly in the Western areas, but also in some eastern local dialects, lose their sonority before unvoiced consonants in the middle of words, and partially at the end of the word: sat (cam) 'garden', *dup* (дуб) 'oak', *zup* (зуп) 'tooth', *город\m* 'town', *kaska* (ка(с)зка) 'tale', *roskazati* (росказати) 'to tell' etc. There are however, isoglosses, which keep their general characteristic of sonority: horod (город) 'town', *rybka* (рибка) 'fish' etc.
- Epenthetic /l/ after the labial in some verbal conjugation: *spljat'* (сплять) vs *spjat'* (сп'ять) 'to sleep'.
- Occurrence of the apheresis[63], particularly in the Eastern subgroup: *za'dno* (за'дно) *vs zaodno* (заодно) 'at the same time' etc.

---

[63] Omission of the initial sound of a word.

Chapter 2

Morphological characteristics

- Case marker of the dative singular in -u: *brat-u* (*брат-у*) 'to the brother'; *sel-u* (*сел-у*) 'to the village' etc. In the Volynian-Polissian subgroup, the ending *-ovy/-evy*, as in standard Ukrainian, is largely diffused.
- Nouns following the pattern of *ljudi* (*люди*) 'people', *hosti* (*гості*) 'guests' occur with the genitive plural the ending *-ej*, for example: *ljudej* (*людей*), *hostej* (*гостей*) etc.
- The endings of certain noun declensions depending on stress. The accented ĕ-reflex is visible in the dative and locative singular of former -ā stem nouns. This reflex also affects the locative singular of the former -o stem nouns, as well as the -jā and -jŏ stems. For example: *na zemlie* (*на земл-ie*) 'on the earth', *na konie* (*на кон-ie*) 'a horse' etc. The endings of the dative and locative singular therefore are: *-ie* (or *-i*) and *-e*.
- All the following speech parts: nouns, adjectives, ordinal numbers and some pronouns evidence a parallel usage of the ending *-oju/-ою, -oj/-ой* in the feminine instrumental singular; e.g.: *halavoju* (*галавою*) – *halavoj* (*галавой*) 'with the head', *taboju* (*табою*) – *taboj* (*табой*) 'with thee/you' etc.
- All forms of adjectives and pronouns belonging to the adjectival declension show in the nominative singular masculine the short ending: *dobry* (*добр-и*) 'good'; *molody* (*молод-и*) 'young'. The feminine and neuter adjectives instead in the nominative singular might preserve the ending *-ja* and *-je* respectively; e.g.: *dobraja* (*добр-ая/aja*) 'good'; *molodaja* (*молод-ая/aja*); *takaja* (*так-ая/aja*) 'such'; *dobroje* (*добр-ойє\-oje*), (*молод-ойє\-òje*). The same applies for the nominative plural: *dobryje* (*добри-je*), *molodyje* (*молоди-je*).

64

- Dropping of prothetic -*n* before 3ʳᵈ person personal pronouns: *do joho* (*до його*) 'to him', *z jim* (*з їм*) 'with him' etc.
- Occurrence of archaic demonstrative pronouns *sej* (сей), *sja* (ся), *seje* (сее) 'this, that'.
- The infinitive may have either a soft ending -t' or a hard (non-palatalized) ending -t. For example: *chodit'* (*ходит'*) 'to go', *nosit'* (*носит'*) 'to carry-imperf.', *brat'* (*брат'*) 'to take-imperf.' but only in -*ty*: *nesty*/*нести* 'to carry–perf.', *vesty*/*везти* 'to carry–perf.' if stressed.
- Synthetic imperfective future of the type: *chodytymu* (*ходитиму*) 'I am going to go', *chodytymeš* (*ходитимеш*) besides the usual analytical forms: *budu chodyty* (*буду ходити*) 'I shall go-imperf.'.
  In western Polissian dialects (Volynian) a future of the type *budu chodju* (*буду ходйу*) 'I shall go' is also possible.

In **derivation** one can note the presence of nominal suffixes: -*uchna* (-*ухна*); verbal suffixes -*ova*-: *kupovat'* (*куповат'*) 'to buy-imperf.', *torhovat* (*торговат*) 'to trade-imperf.' etc.

At **syntactic** level one can observe:
- Construction to express the dative case with the preposition *k*/*ik*; e.g.: *k sercu* (*к серц'-у*) 'heart-dat.' etc.,
- Construction with the dialectal preposition *lja* (*ля*), *lje* (*ле*) (cf. Ukr. *bilja*/*kolo*, Eng. beside, near, by) in a series of local dialects: *lja chaty* (*л'а хати*); *lje ljesu* (*л'е л'іесу*).
- Restricted use of the adversative preposition *ale* 'but', often substituted with the following: *ta* (*та*), *dak* (*дак*), *a*, *no* (*но*), *nu* (*ну*) etc.

Chapter 2

2.3.3. Eastern Polissian dialects

This subgroup embodies the dialects of the north-eastern territory of Ukraine. These dialects include the region of Černihiv, the northern half of the region of Sumy and the northern (left bank) districts of the region of Kyjiv. The southern boundary of Eastern Polissian borders with the Central Dnipro (south-eastern) dialects and runs along the conventional line: Perejaslav-Chmel'nyc'kyj, Pyrjatyn, Konotop, and along the river Sejm, verges towards the Russian dialects. Furthermore a narrow belt of northern dialectal features also encompass the south-western part of the region of Brjansk, more exactly the area around Starodub (Starodubščyna), some districts of the regions of Kursk, Belgorod and Voronež in the Russian Federation (cf. Žylko 1966: 147-148).

Eastern Polissian dialects preserve many archaic forms. They are considered to be the continuation of the dialects spoken by the ancient East Slavic tribes of Poljans and Sěverjans. The Eastern Polissian territory has been reducing its original extension as a consequence of the expansion of south-eastern dialects.

Eastern Polissian dialects do not form a consistent subgroup. They are marked by a series of features and can be further divided into smaller groups. Their southern part overlaps with south-eastern dialects, thus forming a transitional-mixed area because of the interaction with the south-eastern group.

Apart from the uttermost eastern extension of Polissian dialects (towards Russian) whose characterization has been affected not just by their geographic position but also by migration processes (Železnjak 2004: 674), a particular group of dialects form a transitional type towards the Belarusian language area.[64] The Ukrainian-Belarusian transitional dialects are characterized by the interaction of

---

[64] The Ukrainian-Belarusian transitional dialects are situated in the north and north-western part of the region of Černihiv. They cover

66

Chapter 2

Ukrainian and Belarusian dialect areas. Therefore it is difficult to determine the origin of their dialectal basis: these might be either attributed to the Ukrainian or to Belarusian language area (cf. Žylko 1953; Žylko 1955: 77; Bevzenko 1980: 207-208).[65]
Some of the dialectologists who actively studied these dialects include Hancov, Kurylo, Vynohrads'kyj, Žylko, Lysenko, Nikolajenko.

Phonetic-phonological features

- Differentiation between accented and non-accented vocalism. In unstressed position the number of vowels can vary from 4 to 6 depending on the dialects; in stressed position one can have up to 8 vowels.
- Preservation of diphthongs instead of etymological <o, e, ě>: *vuol* (вуол) 'ox', *died* (дied) 'grandfather'.
- Development of diphthong [ie] or, more rarely, monophthong [i] in place of ancient (etymological) [ē] in tonic position and [ē] in new closed syllables: *vie*ter (вie*тер*) 'wind'; *pieč* (пие*ч*) 'stove, oven'.
- Akannja is a widespread outcome across these dialects: *halavà* (галавá) 'head', *vadà* (вадá) 'water'.
- Tendency in specific groups of local dialects to the softening of labials and /č/ <ч> [tʃ] before [e]; /č/ <ч> is tendentially semi-palatalized in word final position: *noč·* (ноч·) 'night', *pieč·* (пieч·) 'stove, oven'.
- Hard realization or half-soft of voiceless affricate [ts]/[ц] in word final position: *otec·* (отец·) 'father' etc.
- A similar realization concerns [r]/[р]: *poradok* (порадок) 'order'.

---

the area placed between the northern part of the Dnipro line (Ukrainian side) and the mouth of the river Snov, including the upper part of the river Desna down to Černihiv. Cf. AUM. Vol.1, map. IX.

[65] The current reality is rather complex and is the object of a special research project carried out by the author.

- Substitution [f]/[ф] with [x] or [xv] «хв»: *chudbol* (худбóл) 'football', *chvara* (хвáра) 'headlight'.
- Preservation of voiced consonants in word final position in some dialects: *zub* (зуб) 'tooth'.
- Loss of the semivowel /j/ on the edge of prefix and root morpheme: *vyšla* (вишла) 'she went out'.
- Apheresis.

Morpho-syntactic features

- Ending of singular masculine and neuter nouns at the dative -u/-у: *bratu* (брату) ' brother-dat.'; *konju* (коню) 'horse-dat.'.
- Nouns, adjectives, ordinal numbers and some pronouns evidence a parallel usage of the ending -oju/-ою, -oj/-ой in the feminine instrumental singular; e.g.: *halavoju* (галавóю) – *halavoj* (галавóй) 'head-instr., with/by the head', *taboju* (табóю) – *taboj* (табóй) 'with thee/you', rukoju (рукою), *rukoj* (рукой) 'hand-instr. with/by the hand' etc.
- Dropping of prothetic -n in 3rd person personal pronouns: *do joho* (до його) 'to him', *z jim* (з їм) 'with him'.
- Contracted forms of adjectives and participles in the nominative singular (although the long form is also possible): *dobry* (дóбри) 'good', *stary* (стари) 'old' etc., and long endings generally occur in feminine and neuter nouns at the nominative singular and plural: *douhaja* (дóўгайа) 'long', *žouteje* (жóўтейе) 'yellowish'.
- Infinitive with suffix -t'/-т' in verbs with a vowel stem: *hamaniet'* (гаманіет') 'to speak in a low voice', *byt'* (бит') 'to beat' etc.
- Analytic future of imperfective verbs: *budu robyt'* (буду робит') 'I shall do/make', *budu sluchat'* (буду слухат') 'I shall listen' etc.
- The following prepositional constructs (phrases) are possible:

- pomež + gen. in the sense of close, nearby (помеж + род. в. у значенні 'поряд', 'коло'), for example: *pomež školy žyve* (по́меж шко́ли живе́) 'he lives near the school';
- к (ік)+ dat. instead of do + gen.: *k bratu* (к бра́ту) 'to the brother-dat.', *ik stalu* (ік сталу́) 'to the table-dat.';
- l'ja/l'je (л'а, (л'е)+ gen. similar to Ukrainian bilja (close): *lja chaty* (л'а ха́ти) 'by the cottage/house', lje riečky (л'е ріечки) 'near the river';
- zaza + instr.: *zaza mnoju* (заза мно́йу) 'behind me';
- nau + gen. (наў + род. в. мн.): *nau kart, nau murku* (наў карт, наў му́рки).

• Use of copulative and adversative conjunctions: da (да), dak (дак) 'but, so, and'.

Lexis

These dialects have a high number of specific lexical items. They share part of their vocabulary with adjacent Belarusian and Russian dialects (southern group). Part of the eastern Polissian lexical stock[66] also has correspondences, for historical reasons, in the Poltava and Sloboda dialects (south-eastern group).

Dialectisms in Ukrainian literary works

Eastern Polissian dialectal elements can be found in the works of Ukrainian literary authors. Features of the local dialects spoken in the area of Brovary (region of Kyjiv) already occur in the work of Nekraševyč (18th c.) which still belong to the old Ukrainian literary tradition. In the 19th century despite the fact that Kuliš (1819-1897), one of the main ideologists and activists in the development of modern Ukrainian, tried to use a relatively 'neutral' language

---

[66] For a list of examples, see: Žylko (1955: 80-81), Lysenko (1974).

in his works for he intended to create a language with pan-regional features, some dialectal peculiarities can still be detected in his writings (cf. Del Gaudio 2010b). Barvinok (1829-1911) also drew on the dialects spoken in rural villages in her literary works.

Polissian dialectisms occur in the writer of fables Hlibov (1827-1893). In the 20th century also Vasyl'čenko (1879-1932), Tyčyna (1891-1967) and the film producer and director Dovženko (1894-1956) turned to this dialectal source (Cf. Železnjak 2004: 674).

2.3.4. Central Polissian dialects

Central Polissian dialects (also right bank Polissian) is one of the three subgroups in which the northern dialects are divided. It is spoken in the northern parts of the regions of Kyjiv, Žytomyr and Rivne and it is separated by the Volhynian dialects by a conventional line passing north of Rivne, Novohrad-Volyns'kyj, the upper course of the river Uborti, north of Žytomyr and Kyjiv up to the junction of the river Oster with the Desna on the left side of the Dnipro. The western boundary dividing western (Volhynian) and central Polissian subgroups goes through the left bank of the river Horyn' and along the latter up to the Prypjat'. The Dnipro represents its natural border in the east. The northern edge extends along the Ukrainian-Belarusian border with some transitional areas. These dialects share, especially in their northern part, many common features with Belarusian dialects.

Central Polissian dialects were specifically studied by Nazarova (1968; 1985); Nykončuk (1979; 1994).

Phonetic-phonological features

One of the chief peculiarities differentiating central Polissian from south-eastern dialects and standard Ukrainian is vocalism. This can appear either as a seven-vowel system or, in some areas, it may have six vowels and relics of diphthongs (Nykončuk 2004: 581).

- Non consistent akannja (o > a in unstressed syllables). Akannja is prevalent closer to the Ukrainian-Belarusian border (district of Čornobyl', region of Kyjiv[67]);
- Relics of diphthongs[68] instead of the original (etymological) <o> /o/ in the historical closed syllables: uo [wo], ue [we]. This feature is today basically confined to the most northern areas of the central Polissian group. One can observe in many cases monophthongs, for example [u]: *kut* (кут); *kit* (кіт) 'cat'.
  A similar outcome also concerns the historical development of [ē]: *siem* (сіем) 'seven'; *postiel'* (постіель) 'bed'.
- Sporadic occurrence of ukannja.
- Voiced consonants in word final position may become voiceless in part of these dialects: *dup* (дуп) 'oak', *sat* (сат) 'garden'. The lenition is also observable before a voiceless consonant within the word: *lexko* (лехко) 'light'.

Morpho-syntactic features

The degree of variation at the morphological level can be observed:

- The future of imperfective verbs displays both the synthetic and the analytic forms: *robytymu* (робитиму) 'I am going to do'; *budu robyt'* (буду робит(и) 'I shall do'. Worth of pointing out is the fact

---

[67] A comprehensive collection of dialectal texts (in Ukrainian transcription) of the area of Čornobyl' with commentaries can be consulted in the volume "Hovirky Čornobyl's'koji zony" (Hrycenko et al. 1996).

[68] Diphthongs began to disappear in the northern territory of the region of Kyjiv already in the 1860-s and 1870-s as reported in Mychal'čuk's materials. Cf. Žylko (1955: 84).

that this characteristic differentiates the central
Polissian from the eastern Polissian dialects.

- Noticeable is the trace of the old dual: *dvi chaty* (дві
хати) 'two huts/cottages'; *dvi vikni* (дві вікні) 'two
windows' etc.
- Contracted forms of adjectives and participles in the
nominative singular of masculine nouns: *dobri*
(добрі) 'good-plur.'; *syni* (сині) 'sons'.
- Absence or very sporadic use of the ending -ovi/-ові,
-evi/-еві in masculine nouns of the second declension.
- No prothetic -n in 3ʳᵈ person personal pronouns: *do
joho* (до його) 'he-gen.'; *u jeje* (у йейе/єє) 'u-prep.+
she-gen., by her'.
- Synthetic comparative forms of adjectives: *sil'nejši*
(с'іл'н'ейш'і) 'stronger';
- Typical syntactic constructions are: *nas žyve troch*
(нас живе трох) 'we-gen./acc. live-Verb 3ʳᵈ pers.
sing. three-gen./acc., three of us live'.

Lexis

Generally speaking, it can be said that Central Polissian
dialects share many lexemes with the neighbouring west
Polissian subgroup.[69] Closer to the northern border they
share a number of lexical items with the corresponding
Belarusian dialects. The reality is more complex since the
dialectal lexis forms specific areas which deserve a further
classification (Nykončuk 2004: 581).

2.3.5. Western Polissian dialects

The dialects spoken west of the river Horyn' (see: map 4)
up to the border with Poland are denominated west

---

[69] See: Žylko (1955: 85).

Polissian. These dialects were related to the so called **Pid-ljašian dialects** which were spoken west of the river Buh and considered until the modifications of the borders between Ukraine and Poland (after II world war) as a separate group.[70] Western Polissian dialects are also spoken in the southern districts of the region of Brest in Belarus'.

These dialects tend to be influenced by the South-western group. The influence decreases farther north (Brest-Pinsk area).

Map 7: River Horyn' (North-western border of West Polissian)[71]

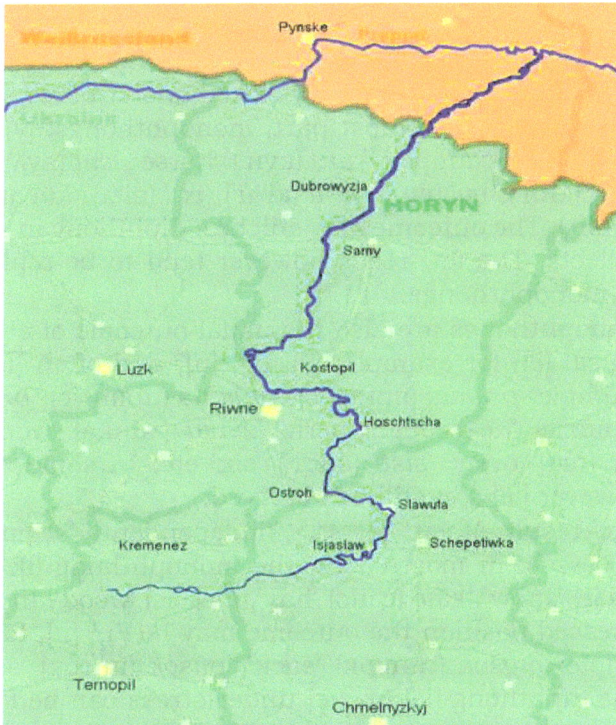

---

[70] Cf. Urbańczyk (1953: 5); Žylko (1955: 85).

[71] https://en.wikipedia.org/wiki/Horyn_River#/media/File:Horyn.png

As for this dialectal subgroup, an attempt was made in the 1990s by Šeljagovič to create a Polissian micro-language based on those Polissian local dialects spoken between north-western Ukraine and South-western Belarus' (Brest area). This endeavour was doomed to failure for a number of reasons which will be not discussed in this introduction. For further details, see Duličenko (1995); Poljakov (1998). An isolated experiment to codify the written language of a single Belarusian village[72] was made by the Belarusian dialectologist Klimčuk. (cf. Nimčuk 2013: 14).

Phonetic-phonological features

The most typical features of western Polissian[73] are:
- Etymological [o] in the new closed and stressed syllables gave, for the most part, monophthongs: [у], [и], [i], [iᴴ], for example: *kun'* (кун') 'horse', *vul* (вул) 'ox', *kyn'* (кин'), *vyl* (вил), *kiʸn* (кіᴴн'), *viʸl* (віᴴл), *kin'* (кін'), *vil* (віл). The outcome may still be a diphthong in some dialects. The few relics however tend to be replaced by monophthongs.
- Monophthongs are also the usual outcome of etymological [e], for example: [у], [ÿ], [и], and often [i], for example: *prynus* (прин'ýс), *pryn'üs* (прин'ÿс), *pryn'is* (прин'íс) 'he brought-perf.', *žinka* (жínка) 'woman', *pič* (піч) 'oven', *šist'* (шіст') 'six' etc. In some areas however [ie] can still be observed.
- The result of jat' [ĕ] <ѣ>, independently from the stress, is, in most cases, the monophthong [i]: *snih* (сн'іг) 'snow', *sino* (с'іно) 'hay', *lis* (л'іс) 'wood'. In non-stressed position the outcome may be /ı/ [и], for example: *myšok* (мишóк) 'sack'; *pysok* (писóк) 'sand'. The diphthong [ie] or [ие] under stress can be found

---

[72] Worthy of note is that the dialectal features of Klimčuk's village Symonovyči, for historical reasons, are ascribable to the north-western Ukrainian language area.

[73] Cf. Voronyč (2004: 196-197).

in a series of local dialects: *lies* (л'іес) 'wood', *tyesto* (т'иесто) 'paste, dough'.

- In unstressed syllables [e], [и] tend to merge: *seʸlo* (сеиʌó) 'village', *teʸper* (теипéр) 'now'.
- Unstressed [o] tends towards [u]: *hoᵘlubka* (гуоʌýбка) 'female pigeon', *kuᵒžuch* (куᵒжýх) 'sheepskin coat, pelt'.
- Velars [g, k, x] may combine with both [i] and [y]: [гі], [кі], [хi] [ги], [ки], [хи], especially in the northern part of these dialects: *roki* (рокí) 'years', *murachi* (мурахí) 'ants', *noči* (нóчi) 'nights'.
- Voiced consonants before voiceless consonants and in word final position tend to lenition: *solotko* (сóʌотко), *solodko* (сóʌодко) 'sweet', *moros* (моʸрóс) 'frost', *sat* (сат) 'garden'.
- Occurrence of prothetic consonants [v], [h]: *hoᵘves* (гоʸвéс) 'oats', *hoko* (гóко) 'eye', *vulycja* (вýʌиц'а) 'street'.
- In some northern local dialects stressed [a] preceded by [j] goes to [e]: *jebluko* (йéбʌуко) 'apple'.

Morpho-syntactic features

The most typical features are:
- Widespread occurrence of the ending -ovy/-ови, -evy/-еви at the dative singular of masculine nouns: *synovy* (синови) 'son-dat.', *bratovy* (брáтови) 'brother-dat.', *dubovy* (дýбови) 'oak-dat.'.
- Ending -y/-и /ɪ/ at the dative and locative singular of feminine nouns irrespective of the group declension: *vyšny* (вишни) — *na vyšny* (на ви шни) on the cherry tree', *lypy* (ʌипи) — *na lypy* (на ʌипи) 'on the lime tree'.
- Use of parallel endings -am/-ам, -ach/-ах and -om/-ом, -och/-ох in the dative and locative plural of masculine nouns: *volam* (воʌáм) 'crop', *volom* (воʌóм), *stolam* (стоʌáм), *stolom* (стоʌóм) 'table'.

- Infinitive endings in -ty/-ти and -čy/-чи: *chodyty* (ходити) 'to go', *nosyty* (носити) 'to carry', *mohčy* (могчи) 'to be able/can/may', *peуčy* (пе^н(к)чи) 'to bake'. Cf. South-western dialects.
- Analytic future of imperfective verbs of the type: *budu chodyty* (буду ходити) 'I shall go' and *mu chodyty* (му ходити).
- Derivation: nominative suffix -ysko/-иско which may also occur in other Polissian and south-eastern dialects.
- Syntactic constructions of the type: *nas bulo dvoch* (нас було́ двох) (instead of нас було́ дво́є) ' we were two'; *meni bolyt' holova* (мен'і́ боли́т' голова́) instead of *u mene bolyt' holova* (мене боли́ть голова) 'I have headache'. Cf. South-western dialects.

Lexis

The word-stock of western Polissian dialects preserves more archaic semantic and lexical traits than the other Polissian subgroups. At the same time its vocabulary is not homogeneous and may have different origins: a layer of territorial words, for example, is Polish.[74] Some western Polissian (Volhynian) lexical features occur in the works of L. Ukrajinka (1871-1913), in particular in the piece (drama-féerie) "Lisova pisnja".

2.3.6. South-western dialects

The south-western group covers the dialects spoken in the south-western regions of Ukraine.

In the north these dialects border with the northern (Polissian) group; in the east the line separating the south-western group from the south-eastern one goes approximately through the following inhabited centres: Fastiv,

---

[74] For more details, see: Žylko (1955: 88-89; 1966: 172-173).

Chapter 2

Bila Cerkva, Stavyše, Tal'ne, Pervomajs'k, Tyraspol', and along the lower part of the Dniester. This group of dialects developed on the basis of the East Slavic vernaculars spoken in the South-western part of the Rus' of Kyjiv by the Dulĕbs, White Croats (Bili Chorvaty), Uliči, Tiverci, Volhynians, etc. Generally speaking it can be said that these dialects, besides their own innovations, also preserve a certain number of morphological, syntactic, lexical and, to a certain extent, phonetic features which resemble former historical phases of Ukrainian (Žylko 1966: 173-174). Moreover, this dialectal group is characterized by considerable internal differentiations due to the complex historical development of the south-western lands from the time of the Kievan Rus' until the 20th century. The presence of various, and often changing, political-administrative borders connected with different European political states and the influx exerted by foreign languages on the local vernaculars determined a higher degree of internal dialectal variation.

Dialects based on the south-western type are also spoken in some areas of neighbouring lands such as Moldova, Romania, Hungary, East Slovak Republic and Poland. The variety of Ukrainian spoken by many immigrant communities in former Yugoslavia, Canada, USA etc. tend to be based on a south-western varieties. A bundle of isoglosses separates this group from south-eastern dialects. This line reflects the ancient border between the principalities of Galicia and Volhynia (11th -13th c.).

According to the classification suggested by Hrycenko (2004: 480), south-western dialects can be further divided into subgroups. Each subgroup covers in turn smaller subtypes. Ukrainian dialectology distinguishes:

1. Volynian-Podillian dialects (Ukr. волинсько-подільська підгрупа) are spoken in the historical territories of Volhynia and Podillia, and include two subtypes:

> the South Volhynian (Ukr. волинський говір);
> Podillian (Ukr. подільський говір).

2. The Galician-Bukovynian sub-group (Ukr. галицько-буковинська підгрупа) is spoken on the historical territories of Galicia and Bukovyna and includes the following sub-dialectal types:

> a) Upper Dnister dialects (Ukr. Наддністрянський говір);
> b) Pokuttia-Bukovyna dialects (покутсько-буковинський говір);
> c) Hucul or east Carpathian (Ukr. гуцульський говір);
> d) Upper Sjan (надсянський говір);

3. The Carpathian subgroup (карпатська підгрупа) includes:

> a) the Bojko dialect or north Carpathian (Ukr. бойківський говір або північнокарпатський);
> b) the Transcarpathian dialect (Ukr. закарпатський говір) can further subdivided into:
>   - Central Transcarpathian (Ukr. середньо-закарпатський),
>   - South Transcarpathian (Ukr. підкарпатський/південнокарпатський);
>   - Lemko dialect (Ukr. лемківський говір).

Because of the high degree of local variation and classificatory differentiations which go beyond the introductory scope of this manual, we shall only report the most generalized features of south-western dialects considered in their entirety. For a closer examination of these dialects and their subtypes, see: Žylko (1966: 173-181); Bevzenko (1980: 208-209); Shevelov (1979: 35-40). AUM, vol. 2. (1988); Hrycenko (2004: 480-481).

2.3.7. Generalized features of South-western dialects

The features which differentiate south-western dialects from the northern and south-eastern groups tend to include most of its dialectal area. A number of dialectal idiosyncrasies display a specifically local character without equivalent in the other two main groups (Ukr. nariččja).

Phonetic-phonological characteristics

Vocalism

- Etymological [o] and [e] in new closed syllables both in stressed and unstressed position > [i], e.g. *kin', vil', pryn'is, pič* (Ukr. кінʼ, вілʼ, принʼіс, піч) 'horse, ox, he carried-perf.,oven'; in part of the Carpathian dialects one can have a different outcome: o > [u] (у), [ü] (ʼ), [y] (и), e.g. *kun', kün', vul'* etc. (Ukr. кунʼ, кинʼ, вул), although analogy may give [i] (і).
- In all dialects, including the Carpathian, the old jat' [ě] (ѣ), in both accented and unaccented positions, > [i], for example: *l'is, d'ido, b'ida, b'eside, l'itati* etc. (Ukr. лʼіс, дʼідо, біда, бесʼіда, лʼітати) 'wood, grandfather, trouble/misfortune', conversation', to fly-imperf.'.
- Intensive or moderate ukannja: tendency to approximate unaccented /u/ to /o/, for example: *ho^{u}lubka*/го^{у}лýбка 'pidgeon'.
- Unaccented [e] and [y] tend to merge: *žy^{e}ve, ce^{u}lo* (жи^{е}вé, се^{у}ло) 'he lives, village'.
- The articulation of [ɪ] <y> merges to [e] in Pokuttia-Bukovyna dialects, for example: *be^{u}ke* (бе^{и}кé; ʻбикиʼ) 'bulls', *žeto* (жéто; ʻжитоʼ) 'rye'. In Carpathian dialects, instead, there is the more central and backward vowel [ɨ] <ы>; for example: *byly*/былы 'they were', *byky*/быкы 'bulls' etc.

Chapter 2

Consonantism

- Phoneme /g/ (г) with its 'hard' and 'soft' realization is typical of a part of south-western dialects, for example: *g'it* (г'іт) 'heat/trial' : *k'it* (к'іт) 'cat';
- Dispalatalization of /r'/ in many dialects. Carpathian and part of the upper Dnistrian dialects make an exception. Compare: *zor'a* (зор'а) — *zorja* (зорja) 'star', *r'ad* (р'ад) — *rjad* (рjад) 'row, line'.
- Devoicing of consonants before voiceless consonants and in word final position: *vidkazaty* /відказати vs *vitkazaty* /вітказати) 'to answer/ reply-perf.'; *važko*/важко vs *vaško*/вашко 'heavily'; *zub*/зуб vs zup/зуп 'tooth' etc.
- Absence of germination (doubling of consonants) in neuter nouns of the *zillja* 'herbs' (зілля) type in the majority of south-western dialects, except in part of south-Volhynian local dialects;
- Absence of epenthetic /l/ after labials in the 1st person singular and 3rd person plural of verbs. This is particularly evident in the Galician-Bukovynian subgroup: *lub'ju* (люб'ю) – *lublju* (люблю) 'I love' etc.
- Change of palatalized d' (д'), t' (т') > g', k'; for example: *d'id*/д'ід > *g'id*/г'ід, *t'isto*/т'істо > *k'isto*/к'істо 'dough'.
- Alveo-palatalization of palatalized dentals: /s', z', c'/ in some south-western dialects, particularly, in western Dnistrian and Sjan dialects: *s'vit* (c"вim) 'world', *z'vir* (з"вір) 'beast', *dz'vin* (дз"він) 'bell'.
- Inversion and vocalization in many south-western dialects of the old consonant group rъ, lъ, rь, lь > yr, yl, er, el etc., for example: *kyrvavyj* (кырвавий, кирвавий, кервавий) 'bloody' etc.

80

Chapter 2

Morphologic and syntactic characteristics[75]

South-western dialects, like all other groups, are characterized by some specific features. These are particularly evident in word formation and inflection.

In morphology one may note:

- Specific derivational suffixes: -anka -анк(а), (n)-yc'a (н)-иц'(а), -l'a (-л'(а) which are not found in other dialectal groups: *sternanka* (стерн'а́нка), *buračanka* (бурача́нка), *vorožil'a* (ворожі́л'а) etc. (Hrycenko 2004: 481).
- The dative and locative singular of soft-stem feminine nouns is represented not by -i (і) but by -y (и), with a further hardening of the stem final consonant: *na zemli* (на землі) – *na zemly* (на земли) 'on the earth'.
- The majority of dialects has lost the intervocalic [j] (й) at the instrumental singular of I declension nouns, and u (у) in post-vocalic position > ŭ: -ojy > -oy; for example South Ukrainian *rukoju* 'hand' [InstrSg] vs Southwest Ukrainian *rukoŭ* 'by hand'; *holovoju* vs *holovoŭ* 'with/be the head' etc. Moreover, in some dialects, under the influence of the II declension nouns, changed the ending -oŭ in -om, for example: *holovom, rukom* etc. Both endings may occur in some dialects.
- The feminine genitive plural has not -ej but -ij/yj: Ukr *nočej* 'nights' [GenPl], southwestern Ukrainian dialects: *nočyj*.
- Neuter nouns end in -e (<ьje) without showing the gemination of the preceding consonant, compare: *vesile* (весі́л'е) – *vesillja* (весі́лля) 'wedding'; *žyte* (жит'е) – *žyttja* (життя) 'life' etc.
- The dative singular of II declension masculine and neuter nouns have the ending -*ovy* (differently from the northern dialects which have -*u*, and south-eastern which may have both endings), e.g. *chlopcevy* (хлопцеви) 'boy-dat.', *didovy* (дідови) 'grandfather-

---
[75] See: Žylko (1966: 182-190); Shevelov (1993: 996); Hrycenko (2004: 481-482).

dat.', *dachovy* (дахови) 'roofs-dat.' etc. Nevertheless, the ending -u is also possible in some Carpathian local dialects: *bratu (брату)* 'brother-dat.', *druhu (другу)* 'friend-dat.', *sylu (силу)* 'strength-dat.' etc.

- Adjectives and adjectival pronouns in the nominative plural have a contracted form: *dobri braty* (добрі брати) 'good brothers', *mali diti* (малі діти) 'small children', *naši syny* (наші сини) 'our sons' etc. Long forms are significantly rarer; they may appear in part of the Carpathian dialects, particularly in the neuter of adjectives, e.g. *maloje dytja* (малоїе дит'а) 'small children'.

- Southwestern dialects preserve various archaic features; for example, besides the pronoun / conjunction *ščo* (що) 'what', Transcarpathian local dialects also have the form *što* (што) that'; the form *čo* (чо) 'that' can be found in Pokuttia-Bukovyna and in some south Podillian dialects.

- The demonstrative (anaphoric) pronouns are: *cej* (цей), *s'a* (ця), *se* (це), *sej* (сей), *s'a* (ся), *se* (се), *toj* (той), *ta* (та), *toe* (тое) 'this, these'; cataphoric pronouns are: *toj, ta, to, tamtoj* (тамтой), *tamte* (тамте), *tamto* (тамто) 'that, those'. These pronouns have their own local correlation.

- In most local varieties, southwestern dialects preserve clitic forms of personal pronouns, e.g. dative singular *my* (ми). These forms are used along the long ones, compare: dat. sing. *mi* (мі) or *mni* (мні < мьнѣ) vs *mini* (міні) 'me-dat.'; *ty* (ти) – *tebe* (тебе) 'you-dat.', *ti* (ті), *tja: ja baču t'a* (я бачу тя) 'I see thee/you'; *vin* (він) – *jemu* (йєму), *jimu* (йіму) *jomu* (йому) 'he-dat., to him' and enclitic *mu* (му): *jak mu ne zaplatyty* (як му не заплатити) 'how you can't pay him' etc. Towards the south-eastern boundary the form *meni* (мені) 'me-dat.' prevails.

- Possessive pronouns may have a contracted (synthetic) and long form: vs *motu* (мому) vs *mojomu* (мойому) 'my'.

- Infinitive is usually formed with the suffix -ty (ти) which is not reduced to -t' (ть) as it may happen in other dialectal groups, for example: *braty* 'to take', *čytaty* 'to read', *chodyty* 'to go' etc. In addition, west of the line Kovel' – Volodymyr-Volyns'kyj – Zbaraž-Chmel'nyc'kyj and along the right bank of the river Ušyca, many southwestern dialects show infinitives in -čy after the velars /k g x/: bi(h)čy 'to run', mohčy 'to be able to', pe(k)čy 'to bake' etc.
- In the first person singular of the present tense the verbal forms keep the alternation z – ž (з – ж), t – č (т – ч), s – š (с – ш): *vozyty* (возити) 'to transport-imperf.' – *vožu* (вожу), *tratyty* (тратити) 'to spend/to waste' – *traču* (трачу) etc.
- Tendency in Dnistrian, Carpathian, Bukovyna dialects, to replace the epenthetic [l] (л) in the first person singular of verbs belonging to the former IV class: *lublju* vs *lubju* 'I love'; *kuplju* vs *kupju* 'I will buy-perf.' etc.
- In some dialects the third person singular and plural of verbs has the non-palatalized ending -t (-т): *vin chodyt* (він ходит) vs *vin chodyt'* (він ходить), *hovoryt* (говорит), *vony hovorjat* (вони говорят) vs *vony hovorjat'* (говорять) 'they speak' etc.
- There are different cases of contraction in the verbal conjugation of some SW-dialects. The third person singular of the present tense (II conjugation), for example, if the stress falls on the stem, is shortened: *vin chode* (він ходе) vs *vin chodyt'* (він ходить) 'he goes' etc.
- The future tense of imperfective verbs can be built according to two patterns:
  a. analytically with the auxiliary *buty* (бути) 'to be';
  b. synthetically with the former auxiliary *jaty* (яти) 'to begin'.

The analytic forms of buty also have two forms: future tense of buty + old past participial forms in -lъ (-лъ, -ле, -ло, -ли), for example: *ja budu kazaŭ* (я буду казаў) 'I will tell'; *ty budeš robyla* (ти будеш робила) 'you will do' etc. These forms are typical in part of Volhynian, Dnistrian, Sjan and west Podillian dialects. The other type of future with *buty* is the same as in standard Ukrainian: budu + infinitive. The construction with jaty: *čytatymu* (читатиму) etc.

- The reflexive particle -sja is able to function as it does in Polish, as a separable word- and sentence-enclitic, and not just as a verbal suffix as it does in the standard East Slavic languages: standard Ukrainian *vin b'je´tsja* 'he beats himself', south-western Ukrainian dialects *vin b'je´ sja*/vin sja b'je´.
  The particle -sja (-ся) can precede the reflexive verb or can be in postposition as in standard Ukrainin;
- Syntactic construction: prep. k + dat., for example: *k tobi* (к тóбі) 'to-dat you' instead of *do tebe* (до тéбе) 'to-gen. you' in some dialects.[76]
- Possessive constructions of the type: maty (to have) + accusative (inanimate) instead of genitive (animate), compare: *maju dity* (майу дíти) vs *maju ditej* (майу дíтей) 'I have children'.

Southwestern dialects, particularly the Carpathian sub-group, have preserved several archaic syntactic features. Some of these features are shared with other bordering languages, e.g. Polish, Slovak etc. Some of the more well known facts include:

- Compound predicate with the copula je (є) which is largely diffused in all southwestern dialects: *vin je mašynist* (він є машиніст) 'he is machinist'; *rika je šyroka* (ріка є широка) 'the river is wide' and similar. Parallel constructions without copula, as in standard Ukrainian, are also used.
- Construction of the type: *mene bolyt' holova* 'me-acc. ache-3rd pers. the head, I have headache' instead of *u mene holova bolyt'* 'u-prep.+ gen. ache-3rd pers. head, I have headache'.

---

[76] Cf. Polissian dialects.

Chapter 2

Lexis

The lexis of south-western dialects is composite and specific. On the one hand, some of its dialects, e.g. Carpathian, preserve a number of archaic lexemes with correspondences in Russian and Belarusian dialects. Forms which were typical of old Russian are continued in south-western dialects and can be found in northern Russian local dialects, for example: *viče* (віче) 'public meeting', *bryč* (брич) 'razor', *vepr* (вепр) 'wild boar' etc. This attests the lexis of ancient East Slavic tribes[77] (Žylko 1955: 107). Other lexemes are shared with other Slavic languages, in particular with west Slavic ones. On the other hand, a certain number of regional and local words reflect successive adstrata of neighbouring languages which overlapped in consequence of historical-political factors.

South-western dialects have significantly contributed to the development of the modern Ukrainian lexis. Many are the words of west Slavic origin, in particular Polonisms. Numerous German, Romance and international lexemes have been borrowed through Polish. Elements of south-western dialects occur in the literary works of such Ukrainian writers as Fed'kovyč (1834-1888), Stefanyk (1871-1936), Kobyljans'ka (1863-1942), Franko (1856-1916) and others.[78]

2.4. South-eastern dialects

The South-eastern group includes the regions of Charkiv, Luhans'k, Donec'k, Poltava, Zaporižžja, Dnipropetrovs'k, Cherson; most of the territories belonging to the regions of Kirovohrad, Čerkasy, Mykolajiv and Odesa; the southern districts of the regions of Kyjiv and Sumy. Moreover, this

---

[77] See: theory of lateral areas (Bartoli 1945).

[78] For more details, consult: http://libruk.in.ua/map.html

dialectal type is also present in Crimea and in the neighbouring Russian regions of Belgorod, Voronež, Kursk and
Rostov (cf. Map 5).
Dialects of south-eastern type are also spoken among
Ukrainian settlers in some areas of the Russian Federation, and more precisely in the regions of Kuban, Krasnodar, Stavropol', along the Volga and in Siberia. Moreover,
they form conspicuous communities in Kazakhstan and
north Kirgizstan.
The northern border of south-eastern dialects is marked
by the line: Korostyšiv (south of Kyjiv) – Pryluky –
Konotop – and along the river Sejm towards the Russian
language area. They border in fact with the Polissian group
and, mainly, with the east Polissian subgroup.
South-eastern dialects are separated from the south-western group, more precisely from the Volhynian-Podillian
subgroup, by the line: Fastiv, Bila Cerkva, Stavyšče,
Tal'ne, Pervomajs'k, Anan'jiv. In the east they border with
south Russian dialects.
The south-eastern group includes three subgroups:

1. Central Dnipro (середньонаддніпрянський) or, according to the classification reported in table 6, Čerkasy-Poltava dialects;
2. Sloboda dialects (слобожанський);
3. Steppe dialects (степовий).

The Central Dnipro (Čerkasy-Poltava) subgroup is of older
formation and belongs to the core of Ukrainian historic dialects. Modern standard Ukrainian, especially in phonetics and morphology, basically relies on this group. Sloboda
and Steppe dialects are, on the other hand, of recent formation. They are the result of migration waves (17th – 18th
c.) from the historical Ukrainian territories towards the
new acquired lands of steppe Ukraine and Sloboda. In the

following sections, besides an overview of the main features of south-eastern dialects, we shall also outline the
Central Dnipro subgroup and briefly represent the Sloboda
dialects because of their historical significance in the formation of modern literary Ukrainian. The following map
shows the extension of Ukrainian dialects compared to the
Russian language territory at the beginning of the 20th century:

**Map 8: Dialectal map of the Russian language in Europe
(1914)[79]**

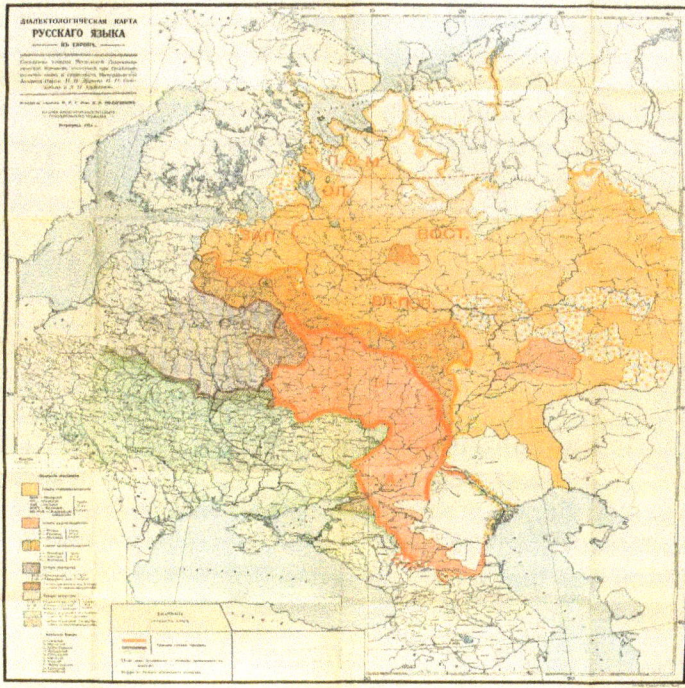

---

[79] https://commons.wikimedia.org/wiki/Category:Linguistic_maps
_of_Ukraine#/media/File:Dialektologicheskaia_Karta_1914_goda.jpeg

2.4.1. Generalized features of south-eastern dialects

For the reasons expressed above, south-eastern dialects are the most similar to modern Ukrainian in their structure and tend to be more homogeneous than northern and south-western dialects. For a more precise description of the most typical south-eastern dialectal features and their territorial, cartographic distribution, see: AUM (2001), vol. 3.

The south-eastern dialectal group covers the largest territorial extension of the three groups. It expanded over the last century including areas which once shared characteristics of northern types, e.g. the area around Perejaslav-Chmel'nyc'kyj (Žylko 1955: 156).

Dialects of other languages are spoken in some parts of the south-eastern territory such as, for example, Bulgarian, New Greek, Moldavian. In the area of Sloboda, Steppe Ukraine and in language islands of the region of Odesa[80] Russian dialects are also spoken. The latter have to a greater or lesser extent been affected by Ukrainian dialects. Some of these dialects merged with Ukrainian dialects, others better preserved their original characteristics (ibid.).[81]

Phonetic-phonological characteristics

The basic phonetic features of south-eastern dialects do not show substantial difference from standard Ukrainian. Variation has mainly a localized character.

---

[80] Cf. Barannik (2001).

[81] See: Some Russian based mixed dialects, a kind of local Russian-Ukrainian mixed speech "suržyk" is potentially possible but it must be restricted to a few dialectal areas. The latter should be distinguished by the Russian variety of Ukraine or Ukrainian Russian. See: section 3.1.

Chapter 2

South-eastern dialects have a six vowel system which basically coincides with the vocalism of standard Ukrainian. Nevertheless, some local dialects may still preserve vocalic traits of northern type. In some local dialects, for example, maintenance of etymological [o], [e] in non-accented position: *beseda* (бéседа) 'conversation', *pošoŭ* (пошóŭ) 'he went-perf.' and similar.

Vocalism

- Ikavism (e.g. in new closed syllable, followed by a reduced ъ or ь) [o] > [i]. This change took place independently from the accent: *kin'* (к'ін') 'horse', *mist* (м'іст) 'bridge', *radist'* (рад'іст') 'joy' etc. On the other hand, in those dialects close to the Polissian area, one can still find relics of diphthongs. This is observable in the parallel use of a few prefixes: do-(до) 'up to/until', po- (по-) 'along/over/on', pro-(про-) 'about' vs di-(ді-), pi-(пі-), pri- (прі-): *dostat'* (достать) vs *distaty* (дістати) 'to get from/ to take out-perf.'. The same can be said about some prepositions used as prefixes: *od* (од) vs *vid* (від) 'from-prep.': *oddaty* (оддат') vs *viddaty* (віддати) 'to give back/to return', *od tebe* (од тебе) vs *vid tebe* (від тебе) 'from you', *od chaty* (од хати) vs *vid chaty* (від хати) 'from home' etc.
- Old jat' [ě] > [i] in all positions and independently from the accent: *did* (д'ід) 'grandfather', *bida* (б'ідà) 'misfortune/trouble', *besida* (бéс'іда) 'conversation/ interview' etc. In a very few cases one can still find the intermediate stage [e] towards /i/.
- Ukannja in some dialects [o] tends to [u]: *tuᵒbi* (туᵒбí) 'thee-dat.', *puᵒžar* (пуᵒжар) 'fire'.
- In some dialects there is no clear differentiation between the phonemes /e/ and /y/ in non-accented position: *nyᵉsu* (ниᵉсý) 'I carry', *žeʸve* (жеⁿвé) 'he lives', *syᵉlo* (сиᵉлó) 'village'.

Chapter 2

Consonantism

In the consonant system one can note the following characteristic features:

- Realization [x], [хв] instead of the phoneme /f/ in many dialects, for example: *хвіртка* (chvirtka) 'wicket/small gate', *tuchli* (тýхлі) 'shoes', *chvabryka* (хвáбрика) 'factory', *buchvet* (бухвéт) 'buffet' etc. Worthy of note is the fact that [f] was originally extraneous to (East) Slavic dialects. This phoneme is still absent in Belarusian and in part of south Russian dialects. It was often replaced by [p] in many historical documents until it became established in Slavic languages under the influence of foreign languages and their loan-words.
- In many south-eastern dialects, with the exception of Steppe dialects, the following voiced consonants: /b, d, z, ž, g/ are not subject to devoicing even before voiceless consonants: *dub* (дуб) 'oak', *moroz* (мороз) 'cold', *rybka* (рибка) 'fish' etc.
- The affricates /dž/ [дж], /dz/ [дз], /dz'/ [дз'] are often replaced by /d/ [д], /ž/ [ж], /z/ [з], for example: *chodju* (хóд'у) 'I go', *zvonok* (звонóк) 'ring, bell', *žerelo* (жерелó) 'source' etc.
- Alveolar or medial /l/ [л·], typical of Poltava dialects, instead of hard 1, which is acoustically perceived as half-palatalized: *holova* (гол·ова) 'head', *moloko* (мол·окó) 'milk'.

Widespread use of palatalized /r'/: *rjama* (р'ама) 'frame', *hrjanyca* (гр'аниц'а) 'boundary, limit', *kobzar* (кобзар') 'an itinerant player on the kobza'.

Morpho-syntactic features

Morphological characteristics are evident in verbal conjugation:

- Ending -ovi (-ові), -evi (-еві) in the dative singular of masculine nouns. In some cases, one can register the ending -u (-у), for example: *bratovi* (братові) vs *bratu* (брату) 'brother-dat.'.
- The nominative and accusative plural of adjectives, participles, pronouns and numerals have the short (contracted) form: *harni dity* (гарн'і д'іти) 'beautiful children' etc.
- Verbal infinitive has the ending -ty (-ти). In some dialects the parallel ending -t' (-т') may prevail: *robyt'* (робит') vs *robyty* (робити) 'to do'.
- Synthetic future of imperfective verbs: *bratymu* (братиму) 'I am going to take'.
- Large use of elliptic (contracted) forms in the third person singular of I declension of verbs: *zna* (зна) 'he/she knows', *duma* (дума) 'he/she thinks', *pyta* (питá) 'he/she asks' etc.
- In the verbs of II declension in the third person singular one has the forms: *nose* (нóсе) 'he/she carries', *robe* (рóбе) 'he/she does', *laze* (лáзе) 'to climb, to crawl'. The latter are typical of Sloboda and Steppe dialects.
- At the syntactic level one can report the use of the conjunction *de* (де) 'where' which often replaces the relative pronouns, adverbs and conjunctions *kudy* (куди) 'where-direction', *jakyj* (який) 'who-rel.', *ščo* (що) 'that-conj.'. The conjunction *ale* (але) 'but' is often replaced by *tak* (так), *ta* (та), *a* (а), *no* (но) and *nu* (ну).

Lexis

The lexical component of south-eastern dialects is by and large closer to standard Ukrainian than the vocabulary of other dialectal groups. Nevertheless, there are also words, which kept their local and/or regional character, even if used by some writers, and were not overtaken in standard Ukrainian.

The lexis of certain south-eastern subgroups are characterized by a number of borrowings from Turkic languages, Bulgarian, Romance languages. In some dialects, especially the Steppe subgroup, one can note a number of old and new Russian words, taken from the adjacent Russian or island dialects.

Elements of south-eastern dialects can be detected in literary works of classic Ukrainian writers such as Kotjarevs'kyj (1769-1838). Features of the Central Dnipro dialects appear in Hulak-Artemovs'kyj (1796-1865). Hrebinka (1812-1848) drew from these dialects but also used features of northern type.

2.5. Central Dnipro (Čherkasy-Poltava) dialects

This dialectal subgroup is spoken on both sides of the Dnipro south of the line: Fastiv, Perjaslav-Chmel'nyc'kyj, Romny and a little south of Uman'. It is separated from the south-western group along the line: Fastiv, Bila Cerkva, Stavyšče, Uman'. The eastern boundary is marked by the Sloboda dialectal area.

The Central Dnipro dialects cover the southern districts of the region of Kyjiv, the south-west districts of the region of Sumy, the regions of Čerkasy, Poltava, the northern districts of Kirovohrad and Dnipropetrovs'k. It is one of the archaic dialects of the south-eastern macro dialectal area, thus representing its nucleus (Hrycenko 2004: 179).

As previously mentioned, the underlying phonetic system, the grammar and the basic lexical-stock are the closest to the modern standard. The vernacular spoken between the Kyjiv and Poltava area formed the basis for the development of modern literary Ukrainian, and later, with the significant contribution of south-western dialects and their literary variants, of standard Ukrainian. Therefore, the difference between the Central Dnipro dialects and standard Ukrainian is not significant. Nevertheless, these dialects also evidence their own peculiarities. Scholars who studied these dialects include: Buzuk, Varčenko, Doroškevyč, Žylko, Kryms'kyj, Lysenko, Martynova, Mychal'čuk, Mohyla, Prokopova, Samilenko, Tkačenko.

In **phonetic-phonology** one can mention:

- The change /o/ > /i/ is not consistent in the northern part of Central Dnipro dialects. Therefore, beside the standard forms, one may have: *kostka* (кóстка) 'bone', *poroh* (порóг) 'threshold'; *radost'* (рáдост') 'joy'.
- Unaccented /e/ may have different outcomes: [eʸ], [ɪ] <y>: *seʸlo* (сеилó) as in the standard language, *pohryb* (пóгриб) 'funeral'; in some local dialects: [e] > [aᵉ] *taᵉper* (таᵉпéр) 'now', *maᵉne* (маᵉнé) 'me-acc' etc.
- Change /o/ > [oᵘ], [u] (ukannja) especially in the syllable with stressed í, ù, for example: *oᵘbid* (оʸб'íд) 'lunch'.
- Non consistent development of /o/ which may also be realized as [a]: *pahanyj* (пагáний) 'bad', *hančar* (ганчáр) 'potter'.
- In some Poltava dialects hard /l/ may be alveolar [l·][82], for example: *bula* (бул·á) 'she was', *moloko* (мол·окó) 'milk'.
- A few prothetic vowels can appear at the beginning of word. In some dialects, particularly those closer to the northern boundary, the prothetic vowel is absent: *ucho* (ýхо) 'ear'.
- In many cases one can observe a softening of the following consonants: /d, t, z, s, n/ + /i/ (which derives from /o/ or /e/).
- Retention of the hard ~ soft correlation of t ~ t', c ~ c', r ~ r'; in some dialects also z ~ ž and č ~ č' before /a/: *loš'a* (лош'а, волóч'ат') 'foal, colt'; 'to harrow'.

---

[82] This peculiarity is also known as softened <l> or Poltavian.

- Simplification of the affricate /dz/ > [z]: *zvin, zerkalo* (звін, зéркало) 'bell', 'mirror' or inverse process.
- Change of /g/ > [h] ([г] > [г]): *dzyha, hudzyk* (дзи га, гýдзик) 'whirligig', 'botton'.
- Different realization of the phone [f] > [x], [кv], [xv]: *chvabryka* (хвáбрика) 'factory', *chorma* (хóрма) 'form'.
- The opposition: voiced ~ voiceless consonants is basically retained. In some left bank dialects, a process of devoicing may take place both before a voiceless consonant or in word final position: *odtkazaty* (одтка-зати) 'to refuse'.

Morphological characteristics

Some of the most widespread morpho-syntactic features are:

- Prevalence of the ending -ovi, -evi in most of the dialectal area. Dialects closer to Polissian dialects: -u.
- Ending -y at the genitive of singular feminine nouns: *soly, radosty* (сóли, рáдости), 'salt-gen.', 'joy-gen.'.
- The genitive plural of feminine nouns may have different endings: -iŭ, -yŭ, -oŭ (-iў, -иў, -oў): *bab/babiŭ* (баб/бабíў) 'old woman-gen.', *sester/setryŭ* (сестéр/сестриў) 'sister-gen'.
- In the oblique cases of personal pronouns epenthetic [н] does not occur in all dialects: *na jomu* (на йóму) *na njomu* (на ньому) 'on him'.
- Infinitive with parallel ending -ty and -t': (ходи ти і ходит'); in Poltava dialects: -t: *chodyt* (ходит) 'to go/ walk'.
- The third person singular of present and future tenses may either have the typical -t' or without it: *chodyt'* vs *chode* (хóдит'; хóде) 'he/she goes'. The third person singular of present tense of verbs of the I declension with the -j stem can either show a contracted form: *slucha, zna* (слýха, зна) or a full one:

sluchaje, znaje (слу́хайе, зна́йе) 'he/she hears, knows'.

- The future tense of imperfective verbs can be expressed with the analytic and synthetic forms: *budu robyty* and *robytymu* (бу́ду роби́ти і роби́тиму) 'I shall /will do, I am going to do'.

2.6. Sloboda dialects

As already mentioned, Sloboda dialects are of relatively new formation. They originated from the settlement and colonization of the Sloboda[83] Ukraine which began in the 16th century, and intensified during the 17th century.

This subgroup borders with the Central Dnipro dialects, more precisely with the Poltava dialects in the west; in the south with the Steppe dialects approximately along the line Krasnodar – Izjum. In the east and in the north they are in contact with the Russian dialects and in the north-west with the Eastern Polissian.

Phonetic-phonological features

- Stronger ukannja than in the corresponding Central Dnipro dialects.
- Akannja in those dialects closer to the Russian language area.
- Okannja as a hypercorrection against the ukannja in some eastern Sloboda dialects.
- Palatalized realization of /d, t, z, s, c, l, n/ before [i].
- Two phones [mn] replacing [j] in words with a palatalized consonant followed by 'a [ja]: *mn'aso* (мн'асо) vs *mjaso* (м'асо/м'ясо) 'meat'.

---

[83] Also transliterated as *Slobids'ka Ukraine.*

Map 9: The Sloboda Area[84]

Map 10: Extension of Sloboda dialects[85]

---

[84] https://upload.wikimedia.org/wikipedia/commons/0/01/Sloboda_Ukr.png

[85] https://upload.wikimedia.org/wikipedia/commons/1/1d/Ukraine-Slobozhanshchyna.png

Chapter 2

Morphological features[86]

- Parallel endings in the following cases:
  Genitive of plural nouns: *hrošej* vs *hrošij* (грóшей і грóш'ий) 'money-gen';
  Dative of plural nouns: *konjam* and *konim* (кóн'ам і кóн'ім) 'horse-dat';
  Instrumental of plural neuter nouns: *teljam, teljom, teljatom* (тел'áм, тел'óм, тел'áтом) 'calves-instr.'.
- Short form of adjectives in the nominative plural: *čužy* (чужи) 'strange, foreign'; *dobry* (дóбри) 'good'. This is more typical of the northern part of the area.
- Absence of the prothetic [n] in the oblique cases of personal pronouns: *za joho, jeju* (за йóго, йéйу) 'for him/her'.
- Parallel endings in the infinitive: -t' and -ty.
- No consonant alternation in the 1st person singular of verbs in the present tense: *vozu* instead of *vodžu* (вóз'у vs вóджу) 'I lead' etc.
- Parallel endings in the third person singular and plural of the verbs of I and II conjugation (probably due to overlapping/interaction): *chodyt* and *chode* (хóдит' і хóде) 'he goes'; *nosjat'* and *nosut'* (нóс'ат' і нóс'ут') 'they carry'.

Lexis

Sloboda dialects share many lexical elements with the Poltava dialects (Central Dnipro), with Eastern Polissian and also with southern Russian dialects.

Features of Sloboda dialects, more exactly those of the local dialect spoken in the area of Charkiv[87], are abundantly reflected in the works of Kvitka-Osnov"janenko (1778-1843), unanimously considered the first prose (novel)

---

[86] Cf. Hrycenko (2004: 608-609).

[87] Village Osnova. Today part of the city of Charkiv.

writer of modern literary Ukrainian. There are quite a number of lexical and grammar peculiarities in his works. A few illustrative examples could be the use of the locative plural with ending -am: po chatam (по хатам); verbal suffix -ova: *rozkazovav* (розказовав)[88] etc.

For a more complete account of the writer's language peculiarities, see: Bevzenko (1978: 76-78); Dictionary of Kvitka-Osnov"janenko's works (1978-1979); Venjeceva (1976) etc.

2.7. Steppe dialects

Steppe dialects cover a vast surface of the Ukrainian steppe and Donbas area. They border with southwestern dialects (Podillian type), Central Dnipro and Sloboda dialects in the north and north-west; with the Moldavian dialects in the south-west and with Russian dialects in the east.

Steppe dialects are of most recent formation as a consequence of various waves of migration which took place between the 18th and 19th centuries. Ukrainian settlers mainly came from the Central Dnipro area, Podillia, Volhyn' and, to a certain extent, from Polissia and Sloboda. Settlers of other nationalities actively participated in the development of these lands.

These dialects are historically based on the Central Dnipro and Sloboda subgroups with elements of northern and south-western types. In some areas, and in different phases of their development, they were also influenced by Russian, Bulgarian, Moldavian and, to a lesser extent, Serbian, Greek and German dialects. This explains a certain degree of heterogeneity. For this reason, some dialectologists (cf. Bevzenko 1980: 239) tend to split Steppe dialects into smaller territorial subdivisions:

> a. Steppe Dnipro dialects (степові наддні-
> прянські);

---

[88] Cf. standard Ukrainian: po chatach; rozkazuvav.

b. East Steppe or Donec'k dialects (східностепові /донецькі);
c. west Steppe dialects (західностепові);
d. south Bessarabia dialects (південно-бесарабські).

For a characterization of the main dialectal features, see: Bevzenko (1980: 239-240); Hrycenko (2004: 646-648); AUM (2001) vol. 3.

Map 11: Ukraine Steppe[89]

Finally, an extension of steppe dialects towards the south-east, outside the Ukrainian state border, can be considered the so called Balačka dialects. Balačka designates those steppe dialects spoken in the Kuban and Don areas. The term itself derives from Ukrainian and means "to speak", "to talk" (cf. Ukrainian *говорити, бесідувати,*

---

[89] Фізико-географічне районування (підручник)
http://ukrmap.su/uk-g8/883.html

балакати; Russian *говорить, беседовать*). This designation originally meant the dialects of the Ukrainian language spoken in the region around the Kuban river.

The term was later extended to mean the dialects spoken by Cossacks living in Russia (Don, Terek, Ural etc.). Three basic varieties of this vernacular can be distinguished:

1) Kuban;
2) Don;
3) Mountain (cf. Russian gorskaja Balačka).

The first variety, i.e. the Kuban one, is the closest to Ukrainian and represents a continuation of the Ukrainian south-eastern dialects spoken in the 18th century.

It is widespread in the Taman peninsula. The 1897 Russian census attributed this way of speaking to Ukrainian or, in the terminology of those days, to the "little Russian language". The Kuban Balačka underwent a process of constant Russification during the last century. Today it is classified just as a dialect of Russian.[90]

---

[90] For more details and a characterization of this dialect, see: Tkačenko (1998); Vasyl'ev (2010).
http://www.rbardalzo.narod.ru/7/balachka.html;
http://www.kubanska.org/gramatyka.htm (13.02.2016).

CHAPTER 3

3. Topical issues in Ukrainian dialectology

In this chapter we intend to briefly introduce some topical issues often neglected in most traditional and contemporary works on Ukrainian dialects. Manuals on Ukrainian dialects tend to illustrate the Ukrainian dialectal territory as if it were a static unit, unchanged since the middle of the 20th century. They do not always reproduce the real situation of contemporary diatopic and diastratic variation, and recent language policy trends.

In the present work, for practical and illustrative reasons, we also adopted a stereotyped approach in presenting the basic characteristics of Ukrainian dialects. Our decision, however, relied on the assumption that the primary aim of this introduction was to supply a non-Ukrainian reader and/or student of Slavic languages with basic knowledge of Ukrainian dialects.

In the following sections we intend to briefly introduce three topical issues:

1) The relationship between regional varieties of standard Ukrainian, dialects and forms of language mix (mixed speech), generally known as "suržyk".

2) The question of whether Rusyn can be treated as part of west Ukrainian (Transcarpathian) dialects or as a separate 'language'.

3) The connection between dialectology and sociolinguistics in Ukrainian studies.

101

Chapter 3

3.1. Regional varieties, dialects and forms of mixed speech "Suržyk"

The strict interrelation between regional varieties of stand-ard Ukrainian, dialects and forms of mixed speech, e.g. Ukrainian-Russian mixed speech "suržyk" but also other language combinations, is generally omitted in most works on Ukrainian dialectology.[91]
This deficiency can be partially explained by the traditional and clear-cut approach to the study of Ukrainian dialects. On the other hand, this can also depend on the fact that the Ukrainian-Russian mixed speech "suržyk" is primarily considered as a social dialect even if it has a regional and, particularly in the last decades, local diffusion in rural ar-eas. Its interaction with the dialectal substratum[92]has of-ten been underestimated in 'Suržyk Studies' (cf. suržykystyka / суржикистика).
It is undoubtedly easier to portray geographic (diatopic) variation without considering overlapping features which would render the picture blurred and more composite for both explanation and classroom works.
In this introduction, again for the sake of simplicity, the dialectal characterization was exemplified as if the ques-tion of language/dialectal mixing at regional level did not affect Ukrainian dialects and their speakers.
The real language situation shows a more complex and changing picture today. If it is true that there still exist small groups of 'genuine' dialectal speakers, who can tra-ditionally be found among older speakers and in more iso-lated country areas, most of the non-urban linguistic land-scapes have significantly changed since cartographic

---

[91] This happens irrespective of whether they are manuals meant for didactic purposes or monographs and articles on specific dialec-tal aspects.

[92] On this point, see: Del Gaudio (2010a).

works and dialectal atlases were compiled. For these reasons, a researcher approaching dialectal field work or even a student who wishes to gain a correct representation of the language situation of a particular rural area, should consider the interaction between primary dialects, standard Ukrainian, other languages[93], e.g. Russian, and forms of mixed speech "suržyk".

3.2. Transcarpathian dialects and the question of "Rusyn"

In recent times there have been attempts at classifying some of the Ukrainian dialects into separate languages. This tendency primarily concerns the Carpathian region of Ukraine but, as mentioned in previous sections, also involved the speakers of other dialectal groups such as western Polissian[94] and the Kuban dialects.[95]

A special problem is that of the classification and status of those dialects spoken in the region of Transcarpathia with extension in neighbouring lands. The geographic distribution of this non-homogeneous vernacular covers: the Transcarpathian region of Ukraine; north-eastern Slovakia; south-eastern Poland, where the local variety is called Łemkowski (лем/*lem* "only", "but", "like"); Hungary; some northern areas of Romania, where the people are called Ruteni and the language *Ruteană* and in the Serbian region of Vojvodina.

Since the 1990s there have been attempts at creating a separate language on the basis of these vernaculars. The

---

[93] Official languages can affect the local dialects according to the geographic position and historic background of the different Ukrainian regions. As mentioned in the introductory section, dialects may interact, besides Russian, with Polish, Hungarian, Slovak etc.

[94] Cf. section 2.3.5.

[95] Cf. section 2.7.

use of this 'language', denominated Rusyn (also known in English as Ruthenian), was intensively promoted by such scholars as Magocsi[96] (1996). It should be specified however that these attempts were made only in the case of Prešov Rusyn in Slovakia (cf. Pugh 2009), Lemko and Hungarian Rusyn.

The Vojvodinian variety or Bačka-Srem was codified at much earlier date (Duličenko 1981: 11-28). The latter variety of Rusyn can be considered as an independent standard micro-language spoken by a population of approximately 20,000 people in former Yugoslavia. These people settled in the mid-eighteenth century in the area around the city of Kerestur. Their micro-language is based on eastern Slovak dialects with some western Ukrainian admixture (Shevelov 1993: 996).

As to the question of the status to be attributed to the Transcarpathian dialects spoken in the Ukrainian territory, Nimčuk[97] – a native of the Rusyn area – in a well-argued article, outlines the origin, development and contemporary evolution of the term Rusyn. He relates it to ethnology, history and dialectology. Nimčuk demonstrated how the ethnonym referred to 'a person belonging to the Ukrainian-Cossack nation' in the documents of the 17th and 18th century (Nimčuk 2013: 6). He also pointed out that many promoters of Transcarpathian culture at the beginning of the 20th century attributed their local vernacular to Ukrainian or, in the terminology used at that time, to "Little Russian" (Nimčuk 2013: 8). Still in the Soviet period, Transcarpathian activists would have been labelled as 'Ukrainian nationalists'. In his opinion a real movement towards a "Rusyn specificity" first began in the 1990s. After an analysis of the core features of his native dialect, the

[96] Magocsi is professor of history and political sciences and Chair of Ukrainian Studies at the University of Toronto.

[97] It is worth remembering that Nimčuk is also a corresponding member of the Ukrainian Academy of Sciences and chief of the department of Ukrainian language history.

scholar came to the conclusion that "if one creates a unified language on the basis of common elements of Carpathian dialects, the result will be an idiom with typical Ukrainian dialectal features". The functioning of such a language would be superfluous since standard Ukrainian already satisfies the communicative needs of Carpathian-Ukrainians (Nimčuk 2013: 13). On the other hand, he encourages the active use of the local dialects because of their historical-linguistic and folkloristic importance. Nevertheless, he does not see the necessity of codifying a new literary language on these premises (Nimčuk 2013: 23).

In conclusion one can note a kind of dichotomy between those scholars claiming the autonomy of Rusyn as a separate language and those linguists working within the Ukrainian dialectal tradition who consider it just as a local Ukrainian vernacular. The latter approach mainly relies on dialectal-linguistic observations. The former, on the other hand, adopts a broader historical-cultural and political approach.

Leaving aside the complex historical and political vicissitudes of this region which created the premises for the claims of the above mentioned scholars and local activists, one can say that the debates about the status to be attributed to the Transcarpathian dialects[98] was accompanied by intense discussions both by those who advocate the existence of this 'language' and by its detractors.[99]

---

[98] In accordance with a well-established scholarly tradition, the term 'Transcarpathian' is used primarily in the ethnolinguistic sense. As Danylenko reports: "these dialects belong to the Ukrainian linguistic and cultural space irrespective of their positioning within certain political entities" (Danylenko 2015: 226).

[99] On this topic, also see: Comrie (1992: 452-456); Shevelov (1993).

Chapter 3

3.3. Dialectology and sociolinguistics in Ukrainian studies

In Ukraine, and more widely in the East Slavic dialectal tradition, dialectology and sociolinguistics are generally treated, with some exceptions, as two separate disciplines, and not as if they were complementary to each other.[100]
If the tendency in western European tradition has been to include dialectology within sociolinguistics (Cf. Trudgill 1999: 1-3), the same cannot be said about East Slavic, and particularly, Ukrainian dialectal studies. This trend to keep the two disciplines neatly separated could also be rooted in the origin of standard Ukrainian. This language in fact developed from a vernacular tradition and was origin-ally a mostly dialect-based language. Nothwithstanding the above mentioned interpretaton the Ukrainian manuals used for didactic purposes are either rigidly based on a monolithic conception of dialect and its structure or are completely devoted to sociolinguistic issues.
In the academic Encyclopedia of the Ukrainian language, for example, under the entry "Sociolinhvistyka", Brytsyn in a concise and well-presented article points out all the es-sential issues of Ukrainian sociolinguistics. Nevertheless, there is no mention of dialectology (Brytsyn 2004: 631; 2007: 654).
Hrycenko, on the other hand, in his articles on dialectol-ogy, published in the same Encyclopedia, briefly acknowl-edges the interaction between dialects and "social dialects" and that the latter are to be considered as part of sociolin-

---

[100] This last section may appear more as a scholarly discussion than a handbook chapter. This is because it partially relies on a paper devoted to the relationship between dialectology and so-ciolinguistics in the East Slavic and Ukrainian linguistic tradi-tions. In our view, however, it was necessary to make the reader aware of this formal subdivision of these two related disciplines (Cf. Del Gaudio 2016).

guistics. He also defines the object of study of social dialectology, and adds that *"Крім синхронії та історичної
діалектології, виділяють діалектологію як частину
соціолінгвістики, що вивчає соціальну, професійну,
вікову диференціацію мови. Предмет соціальної
діалектології – арго, жаргони, сленги, суржик"*[101]
(Hrycenko 2004: 150; 2007: 155).

Rusanivs'kyj in an article called "Sociolinhvistyka i dialektolohija" which appeared in the leading Ukrainian
journal of linguistics "Movoznavstvo", tried to address the
question of the interconnection between these two linguistic branches. Nevertheless, in spite of some interesting remarks such as, for example, the use of similar methods in
contemporary dialectological and sociolinguistic research,
the existence of some linguistic trends which looked with
favour on the levelling of dialects since this would have
meant the full establishement of sociolinguistics as a discipline at the expense of dialectology, the linguist skimmed
over other related topics thus leaving the issue unques-
tioned. Rusanivs'ky, however, seems to imply a kind of hid-
den supremacy of dialectology over sociolinguistics since
in his view "dialectology better illustrates the peculiarities
of social development than other linguistic branches" (Cf.
Rusanivs'ky 2006: 3-7).
Selivanova in her voluminous "Sučasna linhvistyka" (Contemporary Linguistics) deals with the concept of dialect
within the chapter devoted to sociolinguistics. Yet the linguist seems not to pay attention to the connection occur-
ring between these two correlated branches. The only thing
she says to this purpose, relying on Žimurs'kyj (1969: 23),

---

[101] *"Besides synchrony and historic dialectology, one can distinguish
dialectology as part of sociolinguistics which studies the social,
professional, age-specific differentiation of the language. The object of study of social dialectology are: argot, jargon, slang,
suržyk"* [translated by the author].

is that the difference between territorial and social dialects is superfluous (Selivanova 2008: 327-329).

Not much is said on the topic by other principal Ukrainian sociolinguists. Masenko in her "Narysy z sociolinhvistyky" (Outline of Sociolinguistics), for example only remarks that the study of language as a social phenomen was historically related to dialectology in France and, paraphrasing Tyščenko (2007: 71), she underlines that linguistic geography also played an important role in the development of German sociolinguistics (Masenko 2010: 8).

Macjuk, in the section of her monograph devoted to the "question of social dialectology" concisely illustrates the historical framework of the first three decades of the 20th century when some leading Soviet linguists and dialectologists of the time raised the necessity of introducing and studying the social aspect in dialectology (Macjuk 2008: 337-338). In another article she speaks about the interaction of sociolinguistics with other disciplines, mentioning Trudgill's view on the connection between dialectology and sociolinguistics (Macjuk 2010: 6).

Dialectology and sociolinguistics are likewise treated as separate disciplines in Kočerhan's substantial work "Zahal'ne movoznavstvo" (General linguistics) (Kočerhan 2010: 14).

The tendency to keep the two disciplines rigorously separated may undoubtedly involve some didactic advantages. This is particularly true when a student approaches Ukrainian dialectology for the first time with the straightforward intention of gaining an overview of territorial variation. Nevertheless, such an approach to dialects, especially at a more advanced level of research, can also be misleading.

An attentive reader, in fact, in evaluating contemporary dialectal data should take into account the strict interrelation between social factors and dialect variation.

GLOSSARY

Akannja (акання): the merge of unstressed /a/ and /o/ is called *akannja* (cf. Russian аканье). It contrasts with **okannja**: the tendency of keeping the original pronunciation of non-accented [o].

Areal (ареал): an area in dialectology means a geographical region isolated on the basis of its linguistic characteristics.

Diakrytyčni znaky (діакритичні знаки): marks (or 'diacritics') added to a symbol to alter the way it is pronounced.

Dialektnyj masyv (діалектний масив): totality of more or less homogeneous (uniform) dialectal/language features typical of a larger dialectal area (cf. Ukr. сукупність однорідних мовних явищ).

Dyverhencija (дивергенція): divergence is a process of dialect change in which the dialects become less like each other (or diverge).

Konverhencija (конвергенція): the opposite effect or convergence. It happens when dialects become more like each other (or converge).

Dyferenciacija (диференціація: a process similar to that of divergence.

Hovir (говір): a larger formation of local dialects make a *hovir*. The term **dialect** (діалект) is also used as synonym for *hovir*.

Hovirka (говірка): minimal localized dialectal unit endowed with its micro-system and spoken in one or few rural villages.

Intehracija (інтеграція): Merging of different parts into a whole, interaction.

Izohlosa (ізоглоса): a line drawn on a map to mark the boundary of an area in which a particular linguistic features is used. A number or "bundle" of isoglosses falling together in one place suggests the existence of a dialectal boundary.

Dialektna rysa (діалектна риса): dialectal feature. A component of a dialectal element such as isolated phones, phonemes, morphemes etc.

Dialektni struktury and microsystems (діалектні структури та мікросистеми): those segments of the dialectal system such as vocalism, consonantism, word formation etc. This terminology was typical of the structural dialectal approach of the 1960s.

Dyftonhojid (дифтонгоїд): an intermediate stage between monophthongs and diphthongs (Cf. Ukr. "проміжна ланка між монофтонгом і дифтонгом"). They are characterized by a smooth articulation as in the case of diphthongs but their glide is not as clearly expressed as in diphthongs.

Ikavism (ікавізм): refers to the phone [i] which developed in place of *ě (jat') and etymological *o, *e.

Naričča (наріччя): the largest grouping of dialects (vernacular) sharing generalized common features, for example the northern group of dialects or northern *naričča*.

Ohlušennja (оглушення): the devoicing of consonants in consequence of regressive assimilation. **Odzvinčennja** (одзвінчення): the opposite outcome.

Pidnaričča (піднаріччя): a slightly smaller unit than the *naričča*. It is generally less used in contemporary dialectology.

Neskladovist' (нескладовість): indicates the non-syllabicity of a sound (phone).

Pom"jakšennja (пом'якшення) indicates a softening. It is also used as synonym of an intermediate degree of palatalization, i.e. **palatalizovanist'** (палаталізованість). The latter is distinguished from the complete palatization, i.e. **palatal'nist'** (палатальність).

Stverdinnja (ствердіння): the hardening or loss of palatalization of a consonant.

Transkrypcja (транскрипця): the conventional transcription of Ukrainian dialects which was established in 1962 during the 11th Republican dialectal conference. A method of writing down speech sounds in a systematic and consistent way – also known as a 'notation' or 'script'. Two main kinds of transcription are recognized: phonetic and phonemic. Square brackets, e.g. [o], enclose phonetic transcription; oblique lines, e.g. /o/, enclose phonemic transcription. Phonetic transcriptions which are relatively detailed are called narrow transcriptions; those which are less detailed are called broad transcriptions. In the broadest possible transcription, only those phonetic segments would be notated which correspond to the functionally important units in the language – in other words, it would be equivalent to a phonemic transcription, and some phoneticians do use 'broad' in the sense of 'phonemic' (Cf. Crystal 2008: 490).

Ukannja (уканння): indicates the merging of [o] > [oᵘ], [u]. It often takes place before a syllable with accented í, u.

NOTES

BIBLIOGRAPHY

Ammon U. et al. (eds.) *Sociolinguistics / Soziolinguistik.* Vol. 3. Berlin – New York, 2006.

Bartoli M. G. *Saggi di linguistica spaziale.* Torino, 1945.

Biondelli B. *Saggio sui dialetti galloitalici.* Milano, 1853.

Chambers J.K., Trudgill P. *Dialectology.* Cambridge, 1984.

Chamber J.K., Trudgill P. *Dialectology.* 2nd Edition. Cambridge, 1998.

Comrie B. Slavic Languages. In: *International Encyclopedia of Linguistics.* Vol 3. Oxford, 1992, pp. 452-456.

Crystal D. *A Dictionary of Linguistics and Phonetics.* 6th Edition. Oxford, 2008.

Danylenko A., Vakulenko S. *Ukrainian.* München – New Castle, 1995.

Danylenko A. How Many Varieties of Standard Ukrainian Does One Need? Revising the Social Typology of Standard Ukrainian. *Die Welt der Slaven*, 60, 2, 2015, pp. 223-247.

Del Gaudio S. *On the Nature of Suržyk: a Double Perspective.* Wiener Slawistischer Almanach. Sonderband 75. München – Berlin – Wien, 2010 (a).

Del Gaudio S. Die Bedeutung von Pantalejmon Kuliš für den Standardisierungsprozess des Ukrainischen und dialektale Besonderheiten seiner Literatursprache. *Zeitschrift für Slawistik*, 55, 4, 2010 (b), pp. 418-425.

Del Gaudio S. The Russian Language in Ukraine: some unsettled questions about its status as a national variety. In: Rudolf Muhr (ed.). *Non-dominant Varieties of pluricentric Languages. Getting the Picture.* In memory of Prof. Michael Clyne. Wien et al.: Peter Lang Verlag, 2012, pp. 207-227.

Del Gaudio S. The concept of "dialect" in the east Slavic tradition and in western European languages. In: *Aktual'ni problemy ukrajins'koji linhvistiky. Teorija i praktyka.* XXIX. Kyjiv, 2015, pp. 7-20.

Del Gaudio S., Ivanova O. A variety in formation? Morphosyntactic variation in Ukrainian-Russian speech and press. In: Rudolf Muhr, Dawn Marley – in collaboration with Heinz L. Kretzenbacher and Anu Bissoonauth (eds.). *Pluricentric Languages. New Perspectives in Theory and Description.*

113

Bibliography

Frankfurt a. M. u. a.: Peter Lang Verlag, 2015, pp. 169-193.

Del Gaudio S. Dialectology and sociolinguistics in the East Slavic linguistic tradition: a short survey. In: *Aktual'ni problemy ukrajins'koji linhvistiky. Teorija i praktyka*. XXIX. Kyjiv, 2016, pp. 154-167.

Duličenko A. D. The west Polesian literary language. In: *Language, Minority, Migration. Yearbook 1994-1995*. Uppsala, 1995, pp. 119-131.

Francis W. N. *Dialectology: an introduction*. London: Addison-Wesley Longman Ltd, 1983.

Grassi C., Sobrero A., Telmon T. *Fondamenti di dialettologia italiana*. Bari, 1997.

Grassi C., Sobrero A. Telmon T. *Introduzione alla dialettologia italiana*. Bari, 2012.

Horbach O. Polissian dialects. In: D.H. Struck (ed.). *Encyclopedia of Ukraine* IV. Toronto, 1993, pp. 112-114.

Horbatsch O. *Gesammelte Aufsätze VIII. Ukrainische Sprachgeschichte. Dialektologie. Lexikologie. Ukrainische Grammatik*. München, 1997.

Jakobson R. *Selected writings*. Vol. 2. The Hague, 1971.

Labov W. The social motivation of a sound change. *Word* 19, 3, 1963, pp. 273-309.

Loporcaro M. *Profilo linguistico dei dialetti italiani*. Bari, 2009.

Löffler H. *Dialektologie. Eine Einführung*. Tübingen, 2003.

Magocsi P. R. *A new Slavic language is born: the Rusyn literary language of Slovakia*. New York, 1996.

Matthews P.H. *Oxford concise dictionary of linguistics*. Oxford, 1997.

Pugh Stefan M. *The Rusyn Language: a grammar of the literary standard of Slovakia with reference to Lemko and Subcarpathian Rusyn*. München, 2009.

Rieger J. Dialect Atlases (East Slavic)/Dialektatlanten (Ostslavisch). In: Kempgen S. et al. (eds.) *Die Slavischen Sprachen / The Slavic Languages*. Vol. 2. Berlin etc. 2014, pp. 2074-2082.

Schweier U. Das Ukrainische. In: Rehder P. (ed.). *Die slavischen Sprachen*. Darmstadt, 1998.

Schweier U. Das Ukrainische. In: Rehder P. (ed.). *Die slavischen Sprachen*. Darmstadt, 2012.

Bibliography

Shevelov G. Y. *A Historical Phonology of Ukrainian.* Heidelberg, 1979.

Shevelov G. Y. Ukrainian dialects. *Encyclopedia of Ukraine,* vol. 1. Toronto, 1984, pp. 666-667.

Shevelov G. Y. Ukrainian. In: Comrie B., Greville G. C. (eds.). *The Slavonic Languages.* London, 1993, pp. 947-998.

Sussex R., Cubberley P. *The Slavic Languages.* Cambridge, 2006.

Tarnacki J. *Studia porównawcze nad geografią wyrazów. (Polecie - Masowsze).* Warszawa, 1939.

Trudgill P. Dialect contact, Dialectology and Sociolinguistics. *Cuadernos de Filologia Inglesa,* vol.8, 1999, pp. 1-8.

Urbańczyk S. *Zarys dialektologii polskiej.* Warszawa, 1953.

Ахманова О.С. *Словарь лингвистических терминов.* Москва, 1966.

Баранник Л.Ф. Причины заимствования иноязычных слов в русские островные говоры юга Украины. *Записки з загальної лінгвістики.* № 3, 2001, с. 3-10.

Бевзенко С.П. Із спостережень над мовою українських творів Г. Квітки-Основ'яненка. В: *Зб. тез доп. і повід. на респуб. наук. конф., присвяченій 200-річчю з дня народж. класика укр. літ. Г.Ф. Квітки-Основ'яненка.* Харків, 1978, с. 76-78.

Бевзенко С.П. *Українська діалектологія.* Київ, 1980.

Беликов В. И., Крысин Л. П. *Социолингвистика.* Москва, 2001.

Бондар О. та ін. *Сучасна українська мова: Фонетика. Фонологія. Орфоепія. Графіка. Орфографія. Лексикологія. Лексикографія.* Київ, 2006, с. 42-45.

Брицин В. М. Соціолінгвістика. В: *Українська мова: Енциклопедія.* 2-е вид. Київ, 2004, с. 631.

Брицин В.М. Соціолінгвістика. В: *Українська мова: Енциклопедія.* 3-е вид. Київ, 2007, с. 654.

Бузук П. Діалектологічний нарис Полтавщини. В: *Український діалектологічний збірник.* Київ, 1929.

Васильев И.Ю. *Украинское национальное движение и украинизация на Кубани в 1917-1932 гг.* Краснодар, 2010.

Bibliography

Ващенко В. С. *Лінгвістична географія Наддніпрянщини.* Дніпропетровськ, 1968.

Венєвцева Л.В. Словник мови творів Г. Квітки-Основ'яненка. *Мовознавство,* №1, 1976, с. 46-50.

Воронич Г. В. Західнополіський говір. В: *Українська мова: Енциклопедія.* 2-е вид. Київ, 2004, с. 196-197.

Ганцов В. М. Діялектологічна класифікація українських говорів. Всеукраїнська академія наук. В: *Записки історико-філологічного відділу.* Кн. IV. Київ, 1924, с. 80-144.

Ганцов В. М. Діялектичні межі на Чернігівщині. В: *Чернігів і північне лівобережжя. Огляди, розвідки, матеріали.* Під редакцією голови секції академіка Михайла Грушевського. Київ, 1925, с. 203-280.

Глібчук Н.М. *Практичні завдання з української діалектології для студентів філологічного факультету.* Львів, 2000.

Говірки Чорнобильської зони. Тексти / Упорядники П.Ю. Гриценко та ін. Київ, 1996.

Гриценко П. Ю. *Моделювання системи діалектної лексики.* Київ, 1984.

Гриценко П.Ю. *Ареальне варіювання лексики.* Київ, 1990.

Гриценко П. Ю. Діалектологія. В: *Українська мова: Енциклопедія.* 2-е вид. Київ, 2004, с. 149-150.

Гриценко П. Ю. Діалектологія. В: *Українська мова. Енциклопедія.* 3-е вид. Київ, 2007, с. 154-156.

Гриценко П. Ю. (відп. ред.) *Діалекти в синхронії та діахронії: загальнослов'янськими контекст.* Київ, 2014.

Гриценко П. Ю. (відп. ред.) *Діалекти в синхронії та діахронії: текст як джерело лінгвістичних студій.* Київ, 2015.

Гриценко П. Ю., Малахівська О.А., Поістогова М.В. *Український діалектний фонофонд.* Київ, 2004.

Дель Ґаудіо С. *Мова українських мігрантів в Італії: соціальні та лінгвістичні характеристики.* Київ, 2012.

Дель Гаудио С. Украинско-русская смешанная речь "суржик" в системе взаимодействия украинского и русского языков. *Slověne,* Vol. 4, № 2, 2015, с. 211-246.

Дурново Н.Н., Соколов Н.Н., Ушаков Д.Н. Опыт диалектологической карты русского языка в Европе с приложением очерка русской диалектологии. В: *Труды Московской диалектологической комиссии*. Вып. 5. Москва, 1915.

Жилко Ф.Т. Перехідні говірки від українських до білоруських у північно-західних районах Чернігівської області. *Діалектологічний бюлетень*. IV, Київ, 1953, с. 7-20.

Жилко Ф.Т. *Нариси з діалектології української мови*. Київ, 1955.

Жилко Ф.Т. *Нариси з діалектології української мови*. Київ, 1966.

Жирмунский В.М. Марксизм и социальная лингвистика. В: *Вопросы социальной лингвистики*. Ленинград, 1969.

Жовтобрюх М. *Словник мови творів Г. Квітки-Основ'яненка: У 3 т*. Харків, 1978-1979.

Дзендзелівський Й.О. *Конспект лекцій з курсу української діалектології*. Ужгород, 1966.

Дзендзелівський Й.О. *Програма для збирання матеріалів до Лексичного атласу української мови*. Київ, 1987.

Дуличенко А. Д. *Славянские литературные микроязыки. Вопросы формирования и развития*. Таллин, 1981.

Залеський А.М. *Вокалізм південно-західних говорів української мови*. Київ, 1973.

Залеський А.М. Діалектна основа фонологічної системи сучасної української літературної мови. В: *Українська літературна мова в її взаємодії з територіальними діалектами*. Київ, 1977, с. 50-96.

Зілинський І. М. Проба упорядкування українських говорів. *ЗНТШ, Т. CXVII - CXVIII*. Львів, 1913, с. 364.

Зілинський І. *Карта українських говорів: з поясненнями*. Варшава, 1933.

Касаткин Л.Л. и др. *Русская диалектология*. Москва, 2015.

Клімчук Ф. Д. *Гаворкі Заходняга Палесся: Фанетычны нарыс*. Мінск, 1983.

Кочерган М. П. *Загальне мовознавство*. 3-те вид. Київ, 2010.

Курило О. Фонетичні та деякі морфологічні особливості говірки села Хоробричів давніше Городнянського повіту, тепер Сновської округи на Чернігівщині. В: *Збірник* історико-філологічного відділу Всеукраїнської академії наук: праці етнографічної комісії. Т. 21. Київ, 1924.

Курило О. До характеристики і процесу монофтонгізації чернігівських дифтонгічних звуків. *Україна.* Кн. 5, 1925, с. 14-37.

Курило О. *Спроба пояснити процес зміни О, Е. в нових закритих складах у південній групі українських діалектів.* Київ, 1928.

Масенко Л. Т. *Нариси з соціолінгвістики.* Київ, 2010.

Матвіяс І.Г. *Українська мова і її говори.* Київ, 1990.

Мацюк Г. *До витоків соціолінгвістики: Соціологічний напрям у мовознавстві.* Львів, 2008.

Мацюк Г. Сучасна соціолінгвістика: тенденції в розвитку теорії і завдання. *Мова і суспільство/Language and society.* Вип. 1, 2010, с. 5-20.

Михальчук К.П. Наречия, поднаречия и говоры Южной России в связи с наречиями Галичины. В: *Труды этнографическо-статистической экспедиции в Западнорусский край:* Мат-лы и иссл. Под редакцией П. Чубинского. Т.7, Вып. 2, СПб., 1872, с. 453-512.

Москаленко А.А. *Матеріалів для практичних занять з української діалектології з методичними рекомендаціями.* Одеса, 1965-66.

Могила А.П. *Українська діалектологія.* Київ, 1974.

Назарова Т.В. Некоторые особенности вокализма украинских правобережнополесских говоров. В: *Полесье.* Москва, 1968.

Никончук М. В. *Матеріали до лексичного атласу української мови. (Правобережне Полісся).* Київ, 1979.

Никончук М. В., Никончук О. М. *Ендемічна лексика Житомирщини.* Житомир, 1989.

Никончук М. В. Середньополіський говір. В: *Українська мова: Енциклопедія.* 2-е вид. 2004, с. 581.

Німчук В.В. Походження і розвиток мови української народності. В: *Українська народність: нариси соціально-економічної та етнополітичної історії.* Київ, 1990, с. 190-227.

Німчук В.В. До походження українських діалектів. В: *Наука і культура.* Київ, 1993, с.128-152.

Bibliography

Німчук В.В. Проблема українського діалектогенезу. В: *Проблеми сучасної ареалогії*. Київ, 1994, с. 25-47.

Німчук В.В. «Кодифікувати» нові літературні мови? Зберегти й захистити української говори! *Українська мова*, № 3, 2013, с. 3-26.

Панькевич І. *Українські говори Підкарпатської Руси і сумежних областей*. Ч.І. Звучня і морфологія. Прага, 1938.

Півторак Г. П. *Походження українців, росіян, білорусів та їхніх мов: Міфи і правда про трьох братів слов'янських зі «спільної колиски»*. 2-ге вид. Київ, 2004.

Прилипко Н.П. Атлас лінгвістичний/атлас діалектологічний. В: *Українська мова: Енциклопедія*. 2-е вид. Київ, 2004, с. 35.

Русанівський В. М. Соціолінгвістика і діалектологія. *Мовознавство*, № 1, 2006, с. 3-7.

Селіванова О.О. *Сучасна лінгвістика. Напрями та проблеми*. Полтава, 2008.

Сердега Р.Л., Сагаровський А.А. *Українська діалектологія. Навчальний посібник*. Харків, 2011.

Сучасна українська літературна мова: Вступ. Фонетика. Київ, 1969.

Ткаченко П. *Кубанский говор. Опыт авторского словаря*. Москва, 1998.

Тищенко К. *Основи мовознавства: системний підручник*. Київ, 2007.

Тоцька Н. І. *Сучасна українська літературна мова: Фонетика. Орфоепія. Графіка. Орфографія*. Київ, 1981.

Dialect dictionaries

Брилінський Д. *Словник подільських говірок*. Хмельницький, 1991.

Верхратський І. *Про говор галицких лемків*. Львів, 1902.

Гуцульські говірки: Короткий словник. НАН України. Інститут українознавства імені І. Крип'якевича; Уклад. Г. Гузар, Я. Закревська та ін. Львів, 1997.

Корзонюк М. М. Матеріали до словника західноволинських говірок. В: *Українська діалектна лексика*. Київ, 1987, с. 62-267.

Лексика Полесья: Материалы для полесского диалектного словаря. АН СССР. Институт славяноведения. Отв. ред. Н. И. Толстой. Москва, 1968.

Лемківський словник: 26 000 слів. І. Дуда. Тернопіль, 2011.

Лисенко П. *Словник поліських говорів.* Київ, 1974.

Матіїв М. *Словник говірок центральної Бойківщини.* Київ - Сімферополь, 2013.

Москаленко А.А. *Словник діалектизмів українських говірок Одеської області.* Одеса, 1958.

Онишкевич М. Й. *Словник бойківських говірок:* У 2 частинах. Редкол.: Гнатюк Г.М., Гриценко П. Ю., М. П. Матвіяс І. Г. та ін. Київ, 1984.

Сагаровський А. Діалектний словник Центральної Слобожанщини (Харківщини). Харків: Харк. нац. ун-т. ім. В.Н. Каразіна, Т.1, 2006; Т.2, 2007.

Сагаровський А. Матеріали до діалектного словника Центральної Слобожанщини (Харківщини). Харків: Харк. нац. ун-т. ім. В.Н. Каразіна, 2011.

Словник полтавських говорів. Уклад. В. С. Ващенко. Харків, 1960.

Ткаченко П. *Кубанский говор. Опыт авторского словаря,* Москва, 1998.

Фразеологічний словник лемківських говірок. Ступінська Г.Ф., Битківська Я.В. Тернопіль, 2013.

Шило Г. *Наддністрянський регіональний словник.* Львів, 2008.

Atlases

Dejna K. *Gwary ukraińskie Tarnopolszczyzny.* Wrocław, 1957.

Czyżewski F. *Atlas gwar polskich i ukraińskich okolic Włodawy.* Lublin, 1986.

Rieger J. *Atlas gwar bojkowskich. Opracowany głównie na podstawie zapisów S. Hrabca.* I-VII. Wrocław, 1980-81.

Rieger J., Janów J. *A lexical atlas of the Hutsul dialects of the Ukrainian language. Compiled and Edited from the Fieldnotes of Jan Janów and His Students.* Cambridge (MA): Harvard Series in Ukrainian Studies, 1996.

Tarnacki J. *Studia porównawcze nad geografią wyrazów (Polesie-Mazowsze).* Warszawa, 1939.

Bibliography

Stieber Z. *Atlas językowy dawnej Lemkowszczyzny*. Łódź, 1956-1964.

Аркушин Г. *Атлас мисливської лексики Західного Полісся*. Луцьк, 2008.

Аркушин Г. *Атлас західнополіських фаунономенів*. Луцьк, 2008.

Атлас української мови (АУМ). Т. 1-3. Київ, 1984-2001.

Бернштейн С. Б. *Карпатский диалектологический атлас*. Москва, 1967.

Ганудель З. *Лінгвістичний атлас українських говорів Східної Словаччини*. Т. 1-4, Пряшів, 1981-2010.

Герман К. Ф. *Атлас українських говірок Північної Буковини*. Т. 1-2. Чернівці, 1994-1998.

Глуховцева К. Д. *Лінгвістичний атлас лексики народного побуту українських східнослобожанських говірок*. Луганськ, 2003.

Дзендзелівський Й.О. *Лінгвістичний атлас українських народних говорів Закарпатської області УРСР (України): Лексика*. Ч. I-III. Ужгород, 1958-1993.

Дыякталагічны атлас беларускай мовы. Мінск, 1963.

Євтушок О. М. *Атлас будівельної лексики західного Полісся. Рівне*, 1993.

Куриленко В. М. *Атлас лексики тваринництва у поліських діалектах. Глухів*, 2004.

Латта В. *Атлас українських говорів східної Словаччини*. Пряшів, 1991.

Лизанець, П.М. *Атлас лексичних мадяризмів та їх відповідників в українських говорах Закарпатської області УРСР*. Ч.3 Ужгород, 1976.

Мартинова Г. *Атлас побутової лексики правобережночеркаських говірок*. Черкаси, 2000.

Назарова Т. В. *Лінгвістичний атлас нижньої Прип'яті*. Київ, 1985.

Никончук М. В. *Лексичний атлас правобережого Полісся*. Київ - Житомир, 1994.

Омельковець Р. С. *Атлас західнополіських назв лікарських рослин*. Луцьк, 2003.

Сабадош І. *Атлас ботанічної лексики української мови*. Ужгород, 1999.

Bibliography

Чирук Л. Атлас ентомологічної лексики Західного Полісся, Луцьк, 2010.

Electronic ressources

Archive. Available at:
   http://langs.com.ua/movy/demogr.htm (Accessed 10 February 2016).

Dialect. Concise Oxford Companion to the English Language. Available at:
   http://www.encyclopedia.com/topic/dialect.aspx#1-1O29:DIALECT-full (Accessed 27 October 2015)

Dialektologicheskaia karta. Available at:
   https://upload.wikimedia.org/wikipedia/commons/thumb/f/ff/Dialektologicheskaia_Karta_1914_goda.jpeg/300pxDialektologicheskaia_Karta_1914_goda.jpeg (Accessed 09 March 2015).

Dialektolohičnyj bjuleten'. Available at:
   http://www1.nas.gov.ua/institutes/ium/Structure/Departments/Department4/Pages/dial_period.aspx (Accessed 03 June 2016).

Dialettologia Italiana. Available at:
   http://www.treccani.it/enciclopedia/dialettologia-italiana_(Enciclopedia_dell'Italiano)/ (Accessed 04 November 2015).

Gramatyka balačky. Available at:
   http://www.kubanska.org/gramatyka.htm (Accessed 30 March 2016).

Izbornyk. Available at:
   http://litopys.org.ua/rizne/ukrtable.htm (Accessed 07 February 2015).

Izbornyk. Dialektolohija. Available at:
   http://litopys.org.ua/ukrmova/um157.htm (Accessed 29 October 2015).

Izbornyk. Karta hovoriv ukrajjins'koji movy. Available at:
   http://litopys.org.ua/ukrmova/um151.htm (Accessed 07 February 2015).

Izbornyk. Schidnopolis'kyj hovir. Available at:
   http://litopys.org.ua/ukrmova/um155.htm (Accessed 03 December 2015).

Bibliography

Jazykovoj faktor balačky. Available at:
http://www.rbardalzo.narod.ru/7/balachka.html (Accessed 30 March 2016).

Karta ukrajins'kych pys'mennykiv. Available at:
http://libruk.in.ua/map.html (Accessed 25 June 2016).

Kurylo Olena. Available at:
http://www.encyclopediaofukraine.com/display.asp?linkpath=pages%5CK%5CU%5CKuryloOlena.htm (Accessed 01 June 2016).

Kurylo Olena. Available at:
http://zbruc.eu/node/42766 (Accessed 01 June 2016).

Dialekty nemeckogo jazyka – Glottopedia. Available at:
http://files.school-collection.edu.ru/dlrstore/b73c2872-433e-7854-175c-94b0c9156a9e/1007720A.htm (Accessed 30 March 2016).

Linguistic maps of Ukraine. Available at:
https://commons.wikimedia.org/wiki/Category:Linguistic_maps_of_Ukraine (Accessed 07 February 2015).

Sloboda Ukraine. Available at:
https://commons.wikimedia.org/wiki/File:Sloboda_Ukr.png (Accessed 10 January 2016).

Sloboda Ukraine. Available at:
https://commons.wikimedia.org/wiki/File:UkraineSlobozhanshchyna.png (Accessed 10 January 2016)

The 50 Most Widely Spoken Languages (1996). Available at:
http://photius.com/rankings/languages2.html (Accessed 07 February 2015).

Tyščenko K. Available at:
http://journal.mandri-vets.com/images/file/Tyshchenko_2010_3.pdf

Tyščenko K. Мови Європи: відстані між мовами за словниковим складом (Languages of Europe: distances according to the vocabulary composition) (Accessed 03 March 2016). Available at: *archive.ec/C5s9d*

Ukrainian maps. Available at
https://www.google.com.ua/search?q=map+of+the+ukrainian+language&biw=1333&bih=690&tbm=isch&tbo=u&source=univ&sa=X&ved=0ahUKEwj119_2tebLAhUCjXIKHRq5A_UQsAQIGQ#imgrc=uil4osPRbdltgM%3A (Accessed 01 December 2015).

Bibliography

World languages. Available at:
http://www.vistawide.com/languages/top_30_lan-
guages.htm (Accessed 07 February 2015).

Zilynsky Ivan Available at:
http://www.encyclopediaofukraine.com/display.asp?link-
path=pages%5CZ%5CI%5CZilynskyIvan.htm (Accessed 06
April 2016).

Žylko Feodot. Available at:
http://www.inmo.org.ua/history/famous-workers/fedot-
troximovich-zhilko.html (Accessed 03 April 2016).

TABLE OF MAPS

Map 1: Ukrainian and Ukrainian based varieties
https://upload.wikimedia.org/wikipedia/commons/a/aa/Ukrainians_en.svg

Map 2: Languages spoken in Ukraine
http://russia-insider.com/en/politics/you-think-lot-people-ukraine-speak-ukrainian-think-again/ri1007

Map 3: Dialectal areas according to AUM
https://upload.wikimedia.org/wikipedia/commons/a/a0/Поділ_території_поширення_української_мови _між_томами_атласу.jpg

Map 4: Ukrainian dialectal territory
http://litopys.org.ua/ukrmova/um151.htm

Map 5: Subdivision of dialectal area (groups and subgroups)
https://commons.wikimedia.org/wiki/Category:Linguistic_maps_of_Ukraine#/media/File:Map_of_Ukrainian_dialects.png

Map 6: Approximate extension of Polissian dialects and their subdivision
https://uk.wikipedia.org/wiki/%D0%9F%D0%BE%D0%BB%D1%96%D1%81 D1%81%D1%8F#/media/File:Ukraine-Po lissya.png

Map 7: River Horyn' (North-western border of West Polissian)
https://en.wikipedia.org/wiki/Horyn_River#/media/File:Horyn.png

Map 8: Dialectal map of the Russian language in Europe (1914)
https://commons.wikimedia.org/wiki/Category:Linguistic_maps_of_Ukraine#/media/File:Dialektologicheskaia_Karta_1914_goda.jpeg

Map 9: The Sloboda Area
https://upload.wikimedia.org/wikipedia/commons/0/01/Slo
boda_Ukr.png

Map 10: Extension of Sloboda dialects
https://upload.wikimedia.org/wikipedia/commons/1/1d/Uk
raine-Slobozhanshchyna.png

Map 11: Ukraine Steppe
Фізико-географічне районування (підручник)
http://ukrmap.su/uk-g8/883.html

АНОТАЦІЯ УКРАЇНСЬКОЮ МОВОЮ

Пропонована праця Сальваторе Дель Ґаудіо "An introduction to Ukrainian dialectology" орієнтована на англомовних читачів, які цікавляться українською мовою. Посібник присвячено питанням української діалектології – науки, яка найближче стоїть до витоків національної мови, культури, до самого народу.

Автор опрацював доступні наукові розвідки, підручники та посібники з української діалектології (зокрема класичні праці С.П. Бевзенка, Ф.Т. Жилка, І.Г. Матвіяса) та узагальнив наявну інформацію. У першому розділі обґрунтовано поділ загальнонаціональної мови на групи: наріччя – діалект (говір) – говірку. Викладено коротку історію дослідження діалектів української мови, перераховано найголовніші діалектні словники, атласи, збірники текстів. Описано загальну картину діалектного членування української мови на північне (поліське), південно-східне та південно-західне наріччя. У наступних розділах представлено головні фонетичні, морфологічні та лексичні особливості основних говорів української мови.

Особливу увагу приділено проблемам, які зазвичай дуже стисло або побіжно викладено у працях із діалектології. Йдеться насамперед про неоднозначну для україністики проблему суржика, а також про дихотомію діалектологія – соціолінгвістика, взаємопов'язаність та особливості розмежування названих наукових напрямків.

Сподіваємось, що новий посібник – одне з перших англомовних видань з української діалектології – знайде вдячного читача та прислужиться усім зацікавленим українською мовою та культурою.

Щиро бажаємо авторові, Сальваторе Дель Ґаудіо – справжньому поціновувачеві української мови та її безкорисливому популяризаторові у світі – творчих злетів і успіхів на науковій ниві.

Вербич Н.С.
кандидат філологічних наук,
науковий співробітник відділу діалектології
Інституту української мови
Національної академії наук України

www.ingramcontent.com/pod-product-compliance
Lightning Source LLC
Chambersburg PA
CBHW070338100426
42812CB00005B/1360